Building Teachers' Capacity for Success

ASCD MEMBER BOOK

Many ASCD members received this book as a
member benefit upon its initial release.

Learn more at: **www.ascd.org/memberbooks**

1703 N. Beauregard St. • Alexandria, VA 22311-1714 USA
Phone: 800-933-2723 or 703-578-9600 • Fax: 703-575-5400
Web site: www.ascd.org • E-mail: member@ascd.org
Author guidelines: www.ascd.org/write

Gene R. Carter, *Executive Director*; Nancy Modrak, *Publisher*; Julie Houtz, *Director of Book Editing & Production*; Katie Martin, *Project Manager*; Georgia Park, Senior Graphic Designer; Mike Kalyan, *Production Manager*; Valerie Younkin, *Desktop Publishing Specialist*; Carmen Yuhas, *Production Specialist*

All Web links in this book are correct as of the publication date below but may have become inactive or otherwise modified since that time. If you notice a deactivated or changed link, please e-mail books@ascd.org with the words "Link Update" in the subject line. In your message, please specify the Web link, the book title, and the page number on which the link appears.

ASCD Member Book, No. FY09-3 (Dec. 2008, P). ASCD Member Books mail to Premium (P) and Select (S) members on this schedule: Jan., PS; Feb., P; Apr., PS; May, P; July, PS; Aug., P; Sept., PS; Nov., PS; Dec., P. Select membership was formerly known as Comprehensive membership.

PAPERBACK ISBN: 978-1-4166-0747-2   ASCD product #109002

Also available as an e-book through ebrary, netLibrary, and many online booksellers (see Books in Print for the ISBNs).

Quantity discounts for the paperback edition only: 10–49 copies, 10%; 50+ copies, 15%; for 1,000 or more copies, call 800-933-2723, ext. 5634, or 703-575-5634. For desk copies: member@ascd.org.

Library of Congress Cataloging-in-Publication Data
Hall, Peter A., 1971–
    Building teachers' capacity for success : a collaborative approach for coaches and school leaders / Pete Hall, Alisa Simeral.
        p. cm.
    Includes bibliographical references and index.
    ISBN 978-1-4166-0747-2 (pbk. : alk. paper)   1. School improvement programs—United States.
2. Teacher-administrator relationships—United States. I. Simeral, Alisa. II. Title.
    LB2822.82.H357 2008
    371.200973—dc22
                                                                                    2008034875

18 17 16   8 9 10 11 12

Building Teachers' Capacity for Success

A Collaborative Approach for Coaches
and School Leaders

Pete Hall · Alisa Simeral

Building Teachers' Capacity for Success

A Collaborative Approach for Coaches and School Leaders

Preface

Let's take a step back in time. It's not a big step; in fact, our time travel will take us back only a half-dozen years. The location is Anderson Elementary School, which sits on a quiet street in downtown Reno, Nevada. The school isn't particularly striking, but it has a diverse student population representative of the changing educational landscape in the United States, with the 500 students in grades preK through 6 representing a variety of cultures and backgrounds.

A statistical look shows that some 80 percent of the students at Anderson are members of a racial "minority," nearly 90 percent come from homes in poverty, and fully two-thirds speak a language other than English at home. The school carts along the usual baggage that accompanies schools with low-socioeconomic-status populations: Title I designations and programs, a high transience rate (upwards of 70 percent), some chronic discipline issues, and a history of academic underperformance. It is, all in all, a rather typical school.

When Pete Hall had the good fortune to be named the new principal of Anderson Elementary School, such was the state of affairs. The building was in an "OK neighborhood," most students were wonderfully polite and eager to participate, and the staff members were positive and enjoyed coming to work every day. But academic achievement rates were dismal, and those around the school knew it could do better—much better. Even in Reno, the "Biggest Little City in the World," in the glow of the casinos and the settling dust of another rodeo, the quest for educational excellence was alive and well.

Over the next two years, the staff and leadership team at Anderson made monumental changes, both structural and philosophical. First and foremost, the staff universally embraced a student-centered, achievement-based focus. Next came an all-out focus on literacy skills, including a second 90-minute block every day for every student, which extended and invigorated the site's literacy programs. Every available employee was pulled into a classroom or hallway to teach a reading group, and budgetary decisions followed suit: Every available penny went toward bolstering the site's reading program, which included the purchase of new classroom materials, an increase in technological applications, and the hiring of new instructional assistants and intervention teachers.

The school tried a variety of programs to strengthen its collective pedagogical skills and knowledge. Several outside consultants came and worked with the staff, and first one and then two certificated reading specialists came on board to work with teachers. The staff investigated and began to use a full battery of literacy assessments, and several groups of teachers engaged in some early-stage action research projects. At the same time, the school modified its schedule to create time for teachers to meet in teams on a regular basis—the beginnings of a professional learning community.

Initial Results

The early results were positive. After just those two years, Anderson Elementary School, once the only school in the state to have secured a spot on the "Failed to make adequate yearly progress" list for four consecutive years, had sprung back to life and earned recognition as Nevada's only high-poverty school to receive a "High Achieving" designation for student achievement. The story of Anderson's turnaround is told in greater detail in the *Educational Leadership* article "A School Reclaims Itself" (Hall, 2005a).

Change may have been quick, but it was not easy. Growth may have been dramatic, but it was not complete. The approaches may have been effective, but they were not refined. Quite simply, despite the gains and accolades, there was a ton of work yet to be done. Oodles of children were still in dire need of better learning.

The early changes implemented at Anderson were not unlike those carried out at hundreds, if not thousands, of schools nationwide. The staff instituted a slew of technical fixes, solving problems at a surface level without digging deep into the heart of the issue. The gains were significant partly because there had been so much room for improvement. When you're on the ground looking at the bottom rung, up is really the only choice.

Taking the Next Difficult Steps

The excitement surrounding the initial phase of the school improvement process at Anderson quickly faded, and staff began to confront a number of key questions:

- What else is possible with these students?
- Where is the ceiling for us as teachers?
- What more might this school achieve?
- Where should our focus be?
- After all the initial growth, what's next?
- How do we keep the momentum?
- Can we continue to redefine ourselves as we grow?
- What help do we need to accomplish this work?
- Why are we still talking? Let's get on with it, for heaven's sake!

At the beginning of the third year of Anderson's renaissance, the school hired Alisa Simeral to complete a team of three on-site instructional coaches. Alisa's arrival at Anderson added a new dimension to an already-roaring action research project, which focused on three questions:

1. How can we best build the capacity of our teachers?
2. What kind of support do we need to provide teachers to help them reach their potential?
3. How can we make the best use of teachers' individual and collective contributions to our school improvement efforts?

These questions inspired us to write this book. As we began our process of investigation, we communicated with colleagues, pored through literature, and consulted with various other school leaders across the country. We realized that everyone was asking the same questions: not just educators at our school but educators in general.

Concurrent questions rattled around in our heads. What should the administrator's role in student achievement be? In school improvement? In professional growth? In collaborative development? And what part should an instructional coach play? At Anderson, the job was becoming more of a teacher-focused position than a subject-focused position. We had on staff a site-based staff developer, an instructional coach for teachers in the building. It was an exciting time to investigate what that meant and how the position related to the work the administrator was doing.

What follows are the current results of our investigation. We write *current* because as education evolves, information expands, and experience accrues, our understandings of the work we do will continue to change and evolve as well. We'll never know everything we need to know, and we may never achieve our ultimate goal. But the beauty of this work is that while we strive, we make a difference.

We have written this book for an audience of educators, both instructional coaches and building administrators. Although we speak directly to coaches in Part II and directly to administrators in Part III, school improvement is built on educators in these roles working together in partnership, and each partner will benefit from insight into the other's efforts. Throughout this text, we, the authors—one of us a principal and the other a coach—also add our individual two cents to the discussion. Sometimes telling an anecdote, sometimes going into a bit more detail, Pete Hall (in "Pete's Perspective") and Alisa Simeral (in "Alisa's Approach") share experiences and outlooks in the first-person singular. Our hope is that these asides will add flavor and resonance.

We also want to note that various forms in this book are available for download in a password-protected PDF format from the ASCD Web site: www.ascd.org. Follow the Publications link to the Books page, select "Browse by Title," and then select this book's title. To access the PDFs, enter the case-sensitive password *ASCD109002*.

None of the work we do would be possible without the solid ring of help surrounding us. We are forever indebted to our friend and colleague Derek Cordell for his insight, wisdom, and challenges. We must also share our gratitude with the legions of educators with whom we've worked over the years: those who came before us, those who have worked alongside us, and those who are yet to arrive. This is truly the noblest of professions, and we're humbled by the impact a single educator can have.

As we've proceeded through the writing process with this project, we cannot say thank you enough to the wonderful folks at ASCD, namely, Scott Willis, Carolyn Pool, Julie Houtz, and Katie Martin—all of whom have made us not only feel like we know what we're doing but look like it, too. To Pete's wife, Mindy, and Alisa's husband, Dave, thank you for putting up with the long, exhausting phone calls while we pored over ideas and text. This book is truly a collaborative effort.

As you read on, we challenge you to critically reflect upon your thinking and your work; we urge you to continuously strive for excellence; we encourage you to cultivate collaborative relationships; and we commend you for making a difference.

Part I | Opening a Window to School Improvement

Teaching needn't be exceptional to have a profound effect; continuous commonsense efforts to even roughly conform to effective practice and essential standards will make a life-changing difference for students across all socioeconomic levels.

—Mike Schmoker, *Results Now*

As we embark upon the quest to improve our schools, we begin with a look into the world of teaching. Here in the Era of Accountability, where standardized tests reign and the status of public education makes us groan in collective exasperation, opportunities abound. Piles of information sit within reach, pleading for us to put our knowledge into practice. Brain research reveals much about the way students learn and retain information. Innovations in pedagogy offer us multiple proven ways to deliver instruction to children. And principles of adult learning clarify for us the best way to teach our professionals in an ongoing, relevant manner. We know a lot about teaching—and we all know we can do better.

In Part I, we provide the backdrop for our model of Strength-Based School Improvement. Chapter 1 introduces our argument that schools can improve and establishes the overarching concept for achieving this by identifying teachers' strengths, maximizing teachers' potential, and building teachers' capacity. Chapter 2 discusses the critical partnership of the instructional coach and the building administrator and why it's necessary for them work together to guide each teacher on a path of continuous improvement.

1

Strength-Based
School Improvement

Are our schools as effective as they could be? Has any single school reached the ultimate goal of achieving exemplary student performance and meeting every individual child's many needs? If there is a school that has attained this pinnacle, it has yet to publicize itself to a nation yearning for the secrets, the blueprints, and the paths to such a status. Where does that leave us? Facing the cold reality that our schools can do better—and not only *can* we do better, we *must*.

Every school in today's educational landscape, public or private, charter or magnet, elementary or secondary, has the potential to become a pinnacle school. Every school can increase its rates of student success, close the achievement gap, reduce the dropout rate, meet each child's needs, and yield a crop of successful, confident, competent, and well-prepared young people. How can we make such a claim? Quite simply, because every school is full of children, who possess limitless potential.

In *Results Now*, Mike Schmoker (2006) excites us with his talk about the "opportunity to create schools better than anything we've ever seen or imagined" (p. 2). All we must do is be willing to see and imagine ourselves generating these pinnacle schools in our own districts and communities. That a society needs good schools and quality education is not revolutionary thought by any means. In a letter to James Madison in 1787, founding father Thomas Jefferson, who knew a thing or two about revolutionary thought, urged the infant U.S. government to "educate and inform the whole mass of the people. They are the only sure reliance for the preservation of our liberty." And in the late 1830s, Horace Mann, education reformer and advocate of normal schools (the original teacher-training institutions) illuminated an argument still put forth in the 21st century: "Jails and prisons are the complement of schools; so many less as you have of the latter, so many more must you have of the former." Who among us doesn't wince at that thought?

In 1966, when sociologist James S. Coleman and his researcher team produced what has since become known as "the Coleman report," a document with the central tenet that schooling has no effect on student achievement and that background factors are all that matter, the light shone brighter than ever on our educational shortcomings. Less than two decades later, *A Nation at Risk: The Imperative for Educational Reform* sent us into yet another tailspin with the assertion that the American education system is a mediocre operation (National Commission on Excellence in Education, 1983). These reports served as scathing appraisals that upstaged the United States' self-perception as the world's best educated nation.

Data Don't Lie

Even today, international data point out the need for increased output from U.S. schools. The most reliable, border-crossing assessment tools are the Program for International Student Assessment (PISA) and Trends in International Mathematics and Science Study (TIMSS), both of which house their data on the National Center for Education Statistics (NCES) Web site (http://nces.ed.gov). According to PISA data, students in the United States showed no gains in reading, math, or science between 2000 and 2003, barely achieved at the average rate of counterpart nations in reading and science, and scored below average in math. Results from TIMSS corroborate these findings, noting no measurable change in the average math and science scores of U.S. 4th graders between 1995 and 2003. The PISA data further suggest that scores of U.S. 4th graders in math and science dropped from 1995 to 2003 relative to the scores of students in the 14 other countries participating in the study. (Dossey, McCrone, O'Sullivan, & Gonzales, 2006).

Within our own borders, high dropout rates, low student achievement scores, and decreases in other school effectiveness indicators shine a spotlight on areas of distinct need. The sheer number of schools failing to make adequate yearly progress for five consecutive years under No Child Left Behind (NCLB)—1,200, according to a study by Editorial Projects in Education Research Center and *Education Week* (Hoff, 2007)—raises eyebrows from Capitol Hill to the most remote schoolhouses in rural Everytown, USA.

Regardless of your political affiliation or your affinity for NCLB, however, the data don't lie. Despite growth in 4th and 8th grade math proficiency during the 1990s, core scores on the National Assessment of Educational Progress (NAEP) are leveling off well below our targets. In fact, "the nation's report card" is spitting out results that are dramatically *un*dramatic. According to the NCES, between 1992 and 2003, the percentage of students scoring at or above proficient in the 4th grade reading test rose almost indiscernibly, from 29 percent to 31 percent. This prompted the recent barrage of literacy emphasis under NCLB, which resulted in essentially no result: The percentage remained 31 percent in 2005. Eighth grade reading followed the same trend at the same levels, even dipping down from 32 percent proficient or above in 2003 to 31 percent in 2005. In 12th grade reading, the evidence is even more difficult to swallow. Where 40 percent of students were proficient or above in 1992, only 35 percent scored at those levels in 2005 (Grigg, Donahue, & Dion, 2007). No, NAEP scores are not the end all, be all of assessment, but the NAEP still reigns as king of the mountain of American educational testing, and it has produced one crystal-clear conclusion: There is ample room, and a dramatic need, for school improvement.

Change: The Nature of the Business

There is no shortage of literature available to school leaders, politicians, and citizens touting the very secrets to school success that we seek. If only it were that simple. As Zmuda, Kuklis, and Kline (2004), no strangers to school improvement, poignantly ask, "If we know better, why don't we do better?" (p. 5). The gap between knowing and doing is more famously vast in education than in any other profession. Think about it: In what other line of work could you walk into the place of business and not really discern whether it's 2008 or 1908? In a jabbing piece for *Time* magazine, Wallis and Steptoe (2006) posit, "Kids spend much of the day as their great-grandparents once did: sitting in rows, listening to teachers lecture, scribbling notes by hand, reading from textbooks that are out of date by the time they are printed" (p. 50).

While society has evolved (read: wireless phone technology, wider Internet access, intensive brain research, and so on), school responses have lagged, sometimes with heels dug deep in the trenches of tradition and comfortable experience. Yet everything about education screams, "Change now!" Students enter our schools with the primary purpose of getting in, getting smart, and getting out. Class rosters change, sometimes daily. Curricula change, federal mandates change, laws change, textbooks change, instructional styles change. Our understanding of learning changes as we take in research-based findings on how the brain develops and processes information. The world has become both broader and more accessible, and the global market demands new and different skills from both workers and consumers. In short, everything changes. So why aren't we, in education, changing?

Conventional wisdom, centuries of experience, and countless research studies provide us with reams of excuses: Change is difficult; change is scary; mandated change strips us of our power; change implies a devaluation of our current teaching practices; change challenges our competence; change adds to the workload; a previous change brought disappointing results; we wonder if the change is really necessary; change alters relationships; the risk of change is greater than the risk of staying put; historically, change has often had spurious origins; and change yanks us into the unknown (Bellinger, 2004; Fullan, 2003; Richardson, 1998; Schuler, 2003; Wasley, 1992). Nevertheless, common sense tells us that in order to improve, we must change. Insanity has been defined as doing the same thing over and over again and expecting different results. Change, then, is a prerequisite of improvement.

A reasonable first step is to embrace Fullan's realistic advice: "We can begin by not trying to resist the irresistible, which is relentless change" (2003, p. 24). We must step beyond merely welcoming the notion of change and accepting its presence as a constant reality; we must become active agents of change, creating it and nurturing the rate at which our context changes. We must mold the changes to create new, better, more positive realities. If we want better schools, we must act accordingly.

The Root of All Evil?

The education system is accountable to the greater society on a number of levels. For the time being, we are going to concentrate our attention on four key levels of public accountability:

1. *Input.* Are we providing an appropriate and challenging curriculum? Are we offering a high-quality educational experience? Are we welcoming our community's students into a positive environment of schooling?

2. *Effectiveness.* Are our students meeting basic proficiency levels in core subjects? Are our students learning what they are supposed to be learning?

3. *Output.* Are our graduates ready to enter the real world as productive citizens? Do our graduates have the skills, knowledge, and attitudes needed to contribute to and thrive in our society?

4. *Fiscal management.* Are we using our funds and resources wisely? Is the citizenry getting a reasonable rate of return on its educational investments?

The fourth level of public accountability listed is an often-debated subject in both public and private spheres. Government halls and neighborhood barbecues ring with discourse about education funding, and with good reason: The administration of education funds determines the success of the first three levels. If we spend our money well, we should be able to demonstrate growth, progress, and success in our input, effectiveness, and output.

Schools with high percentages of disadvantaged, or poor, students receive Title I funding, which is federal money distributed to schools for programs for targeted students (just those who are eligible for receiving free or reduced-price meals) or schoolwide programs for all students (which generally occurs when the student poverty rate is quite high). For 2008, the U.S. Department of Education's budget for Title I funding was $1.5 billion (Hoff, 2007), a hefty sum. The voting public quite understandably needs assurance that this money is being wisely spent.

Still, school districts and state departments of education decry the lack of funding. Every year, there is a call for increased education spending. Yet in 2005 alone, U.S. education spending surged beyond the $300 billion mark. Again, with that high a bill, it makes sense for us to demonstrate our fiscal responsibility.

Underperforming schools receive additional monies, usually in the name of school improvement, reform acts, or other grant-tied funds. These millions are intended to help schools drag themselves out of the quagmire of underachievement. But how are the schools actually using this money? And, more pointedly, is the money resulting in higher student achievement? Are the schools meeting the first three levels of public accountability? Is the influx of funding indeed effecting positive change?

There's No Silver Bullet

When money is introduced to our schools, we often react with, "Ooh, what can we spend it on?" rather than, "Perfect—we've needed another $10,000 to fully fund our professional development plan in math." And when we are asked for innovative thinking, we work backward: The windfall precedes a session of frantic brainstorming, rather than the other way around. We should have our ideas laid out and ready to go, constantly seeking ways to fund and deliver.

As school or district leaders, we have done some of our most unimaginative work in the very situations that require us to be at our focused, creative, intuitive best. Where we have needed to be calculating trailblazers, we have instead opted to follow the beaten path, preferring the comfort of the familiar over the vast unknown even though research, professional judgment, and common sense urge us to do otherwise. When facing a challenge, we look for a panacea—a golden ticket—that can answer our urgent needs. Usually, we take hold of a technical "fix," something we can do right now to solve the problem, when in reality what we need is to embrace an adaptive change. The challenge, outlined by Ronald A. Heifetz in *Leadership Without Easy Answers* (1994), is to change the philosophical mind-set of the stakeholders. We have to discover, and then embrace, what is really the most important thing.

Gambling vs. Stewardship

Ultimately, principals and school leadership teams have to determine how to spend their resources and how to make the appropriate changes to improve education in their schools. Choosing to fund *stuff* or *programs*—and hoping these will be the solution to the school's problems—is a gamble, albeit one that many of us are taking. A single stroll through the vendor exhibit hall at any major education conference does a lot to explain why. Educators have been bombarded by the latest gizmos, gadgets, comprehensive programs, curricula, materials, and doohickeys for decades. Between NCLB and the furor over standards, achievement, and accountability, the stakes are high—not just for students and educators but for vendors, too. Many of the items in question are worth investigating, and some may benefit a number of children. But when we stop to think about our mission, is this *stuff* what makes a difference in education? Is a computer program going to radically affect the academic achievement of any individual school? Is an integrated curriculum created in Florida going to match the needs of students in a school in Maine? Where is our money best spent? How are we going to create the most meaningful and positive change? And, if we're going to gamble, where are the best odds of winning this wager?

Thus far, what consistent successes do we have to point out? We've become a profession of fads, latching onto the latest and greatest new program, idea, or thingamabob that carries guaranteed, "research-based" successes. Stacks of material related to obsolete fads gather dust in supply closets as districts and schools rush to spend more money getting their teachers up to speed on the latest fad. When the money runs out for that fad, we change our focus and seize the next published "savior."

For decades, responding to the federal government, state departments of education, school districts, and public sentiment, we have mandated change. In the eye of the hurricane of research-based schoolwide comprehensive programs, we have felt that each change we've embarked on would be meaningful and productive. But these whole-school reform models provide only "imported coherence," argues Michael Fullan (2003, p. 26). He continues, "People should be seeking ideas that help them develop their own thinking rather than programs." We've seen this with the overly prescriptive models like Success for All and even the U.S. Department of Education's homegrown Reading First. Teachers suppress their creative intellect and ignore their prior training in order to follow a lockstep, one-size-fits-all instructional program.

The effect that this approach to school improvement has on the teachers and educators in the trenches is that it creates resistance to change, which is counterproductive, because change is a prerequisite for improvement. Why tackle a fad that won't likely develop past its own infancy? Teachers are more likely to wait for the swinging of the education policy pendulum with which they are all too familiar. "This too shall pass," they say. "This is the same thing we did 20 years ago. We can wait this out."

In this high-stakes gamble, it appears we have been rather misguided in placing our bets. Rather than focusing on the heart of our mission—the instruction, growth, education, and development of our students—we've been rolling the dice on the fringes. As stewards of not only a gigantic chunk of change but also a significant portion of the population (50 million students were enrolled in U.S. public education in 2006), we must be more accountable with our resources.

Pete's Perspective

A few years ago, while I was serving on the Nevada Governor's Commission on Excellence in Education, I had the opportunity to review proposals from more than 100 schools requesting additional funding. Through Senate Bill 404, signed in 2005, the State of Nevada had apportioned $91.9 million to fund creative and innovative attempts to reform education at the schoolhouse level. Governor Guinn, himself a former educator, had essentially opened the door for schools, districts, and their leadership teams to try new approaches they believed would work for their students. Also included in the process was the creation of a bank of worthwhile ideas—ideas of "Innovation and the Prevention of Remediation" on which other schools could draw.

In order to receive funding, a school was required to complete a lengthy application, which included a plan for implementing an innovative strategy that would reduce the need to offer remediation services to students. Schools' proposals earned more points if their plan was feasible and linked to their Site Improvement Plan, and the funding ratios were tied to the number of points each proposal earned.

As the proposals poured in and I pored over them, I began to cringe. Though some plans were remarkably well thought out, comprehensive, and innovative, others were desperately bland and requested the money to fund . . . you guessed it, *stuff*—a new out-of-the-box curriculum, a new software system, a catch-all improvement program. Then, the coup de grace: The unfunded schools had an opportunity to resubmit their proposals after the first round, and rather than go back to their strategic plans and identify some creative ways to raise student achievement, they doctored their Site Improvement Plans to include the need for the very same stuff! All to earn more points on the proposal's scoring formula—but with just a wispy strand connecting their plan to possible student growth.

The Not-So-Secret Secret

What does the research say about what successful, effective schools and districts are doing to make their gains? If we are going to focus on the educational growth and development of our students, where do we start? Where do we direct our energy in order to address the first three areas of education's public accountability charge (input, effectiveness, and output)? The answer is startlingly simple: We must improve teacher quality.

Although the teacher quality factor is frequently covered in intellectual conversation regarding student achievement, it remains bizarrely unaddressed in most comprehensive school reform initiatives, in which the search for salvation begins at an online store, a publisher's warehouse, or a vendor exhibit hall. Ideally, that first quest for a solution should have an inward focus. District administrators, school leadership teams, public officials, and anyone else interested in increased student achievement should turn their lens to the most basic element of schooling: the teachers themselves.

Research has long supported the claim that better teachers lead to higher student achievement. One study showed that children assigned to effective teachers for three years in a row scored an average of 49 percentile points higher on standardized assessments than those assigned consecutively to three poor teachers (Jordan, Mendro, & Weersinghe, 1997). A study in Cincinnati, Ohio, found that teachers rated highest also showed the greatest gains in their students' proficiency exams; the opposite was true for teachers with low ratings (Miner, 2005/2006).

Some well-known educational experts have weighed in on the debate. Rick DuFour and Bob Eaker, the architects of the professional learning communities (PLC) concept, state flatly, "Schools are effective because of their teachers" (1998, p. 206). Charlotte Danielson, creator of the indispensable Framework for Professional Practice, echoes the sentiment: "High-level learning by students requires high-level instruction by their teachers" (2007, p. 15). Renowned educational researcher Robert J. Marzano concludes, "Regardless of the research basis, it is clear that effective teachers have a profound influence on student achievement and ineffective teachers do not. In fact, ineffective teachers might actually impede the learning of their students" (2003, p. 75). And Mike Schmoker, never one to beat around the bush, offers us this: "The single greatest determinant of learning is not socioeconomic factors or funding levels. It is instruction" (2006, p. 7).

The X Factor

Imagine, if you will, a garden-variety school classroom. It could be an elementary school or a high school; it could be public or private; it could be charter or magnet; it could be new or established; it could be in a poor or affluent neighborhood. First, turn off the electricity and eliminate all that technology—no computer, no DVDs. Now, remove the books. Take out the desks, the paper, the chairs, and the crayons. Picture the room barren of furniture and materials. How will the students learn? How will they grow and develop as thinkers, understand the concept of onset and rime, and make meaning of the scientific method, the writing process, the Pythagorean theorem, and the role of chlorophyll in photosynthesis?

More than likely, you have a relatively simple, succinct answer to the question of how the students would learn: The students and teacher would find a way to continue their learning by working together. Due to the innate craving to learn and the enthusiasm with which we were all endowed at birth, the paucity of materials provides challenges to overcome, not a complete roadblock. If students so desire, they will continue to learn.

Now, for the final step in this exercise, consider that same classroom. This time, remove the teacher.

No teacher?

No more learning.

Hurry and put the teacher back in the classroom—a classroom without a teacher isn't just a place in which no learning occurs; it's dangerous.

Silly, isn't it, that it's that obvious, that simple, and that elemental. We're not overstating the point when we say that teachers matter. Good teachers matter. The quality of the teacher is the "X factor." Everything in education depends on it.

We're willing to admit that the argument is not new. Witness this 1909 quote from the American Association for the Advancement of Science: "Given a good teacher, and locate him in a cellar, an attic, or a barn, and the strong students of the institution will beat a path to his door. Given a weak teacher and surround him with the finest array of equipment that money can buy, and permit the students to choose, as in the elective courses, and his class room will echo its own emptiness" (p. 787).

To truly make a dent in the outer shell of school improvement, we need to come to grips with the simple, elegant reality that it's the teachers that matter most. They determine each child's wins and losses, establish the standards and expectations within each class and grade level, and ultimately influence the success of the educational process. Teachers are the field agents of educational change. Therefore, we must concentrate our efforts on building teachers' capacity with a concept we've dubbed Strength-Based School Improvement.

An Idea for Today's Times

What's revolutionary about the concept of Strength-Based School Improvement? For decades, and maybe even centuries, we've been brainwashed into thinking we need to treat everyone the same. Equity, fairness, self-esteem, negotiated agreements, teachers unions, and the status quo have all banded together to ensure that we shepherd all the flock in the same way: identical treatment for identical beasts.

But teachers aren't beasts; they're unique humans, and nobody likes to be treated like "the next guy"—because nobody *is* like the next guy. We all prefer to be noticed for our special qualities and given a bit of special attention. That's why we like birthday cards with handwritten messages in them, the cashier at the grocery store who remembers our name, and specific compliments from loved ones. Not only does every unique and special carbon-based life-form in your school appreciate unique and special treatment, each one *needs* individualized handling. It is the equivalent of educational malpractice for us to usher all our teachers into neat rows, robotically interacting with them with nary a thought to the gifts they bring to their classrooms. Sadly, that's what we've been doing in essence as we've advanced the philosophy of uniformity and blandness in our educational leadership roles.

As school leaders, it is our obligation to provide that special attention to all teachers' unique attributes and qualities: their talents, goals, fears, experiences, thoughts, and ideas. With Strength-Based School Improvement, that's what we do. And we not only recognize and celebrate these strengths, we maximize them. *Maximization* involves the concerted work of identifying the strengths and talents of each individual teacher. In other words, we put teachers into positions that make the best use of their talents, and then we work to help them improve their performance and reach their potential.

It's a subtle but significant philosophical approach: focusing on strengths and potential rather than succumbing to the more common deficit model. Instead of identifying areas of weakness, lamenting the lack of resources, and isolating points of failure, Strength-Based School Improvement recognizes what strengths a school possesses, what assets reside within its walls, and what successes it can build upon. Rather than pummeling ourselves by counting our losses, we begin to bolster our position by tallying our wins.

The goals of the strength-based philosophy are simple:

• Maximize the skill, potential, and self-reflective abilities of each individual teacher on staff.

• Recognize and individualize the unique supervision, professional development, and evaluation needs of each individual teacher on staff.

• Strengthen the collaborative relationships of the entire teaching corps.

Teachers are, after all, *every* school's most important strength. When we build their capacity for success, we improve our schools.

Who's in Charge Here?

The responsibilities of the practice of Strength-Based School Improvement rest on the mighty shoulders of those in leadership roles at the school level. These site-specific leaders generally fall into two categories: coaches and administrators. (We will use these terms for simplicity, though we understand these roles may go by other job titles.)

Coaches include instructional coaches, literacy coordinators, department chairs, grade-level representatives, mentors, teacher-leaders, or any other site-based staff developers. They possess the ability to approach each teacher and provide nonthreatening, meaningful feedback in an individualized collaborative coaching model.

Administrators include principals, assistant principals, and those in any other site-based administrative position responsible for the supervision and evaluation of teachers. Although administrators' feedback inherently packs more wallop, followers of the Strength-Based model will ensure the establishment of a trusting relationship bent on maximizing teacher potential and having a positive impact on student learning.

Truly effective school leaders, whether coaches or administrators, engage in behaviors and possess characteristics that assist them in this venture. In the next chapter, we will delineate both the distinct and overlapping responsibilities of the coach and administrator as they relate to Strength-Based School Improvement. Meaningful, positive change—a necessary condition for school improvement—is only possible within such a framework of cooperation and collaboration. The coach and the administrator are partners through and through as they undertake this critical work.

2

The Coach–Administrator Partnership

When Strength-Based School Improvement is done right, there is a strong and viable collaboration between the school administrator and the instructional coach. Although there are some pretty clear-cut role boundaries each must respect if they hope to create positive change, there are also some significant similarities between the two positions. More than anything else—and we hope to emphasize this point enough that it takes hold—the coach and the administrator are partners in this venture, not adversaries. They work together. And quite clearly, both have the same ultimate goal: school improvement.

Relationship Triangulation

James Comer (1995) said it best: "No significant learning occurs without a significant relationship." It is commonly believed that because one works in the realm of education, one is open to learning new things. Unfortunately, this is not always the case. Often, educators are even more resistant to tackling something new, which is ironic, really, when one of the primary purposes of education is to teach students to value learning. So how do we counteract naturally resistant tendencies and bring about meaningful, lasting progress in education today? The answer is in forming *significant* relationships.

Consider Figure 2.1. With the teacher in the center of the triangle, we note three clear sets of connections: (1) the teacher's strong peer relationships, grounded in the foundation of the PLC framework; (2) the teacher's strong relationship with the instructional coach; and (3) the teacher's strong relationship with the school administrator. With all these relationships in place, there is virtual assurance that the teacher will be bent on learning, be keyed into self-reflection, and interdependently receive support that leads to continuous professional growth. These three unyielding elements are the critical pieces of Strength-Based School Improvement.

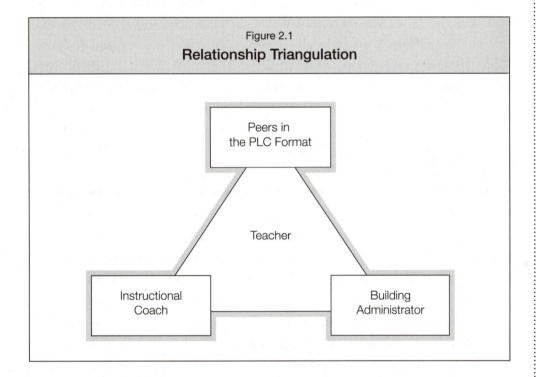

Figure 2.1
Relationship Triangulation

The PLC Concept

One way to set a school up for success is to implement the PLC concept. Spawned by the work of Susan J. Rosenholtz (1989) and popularized by Rick DuFour and Bob Eaker (1998), it provides a proven, commonsense structure in which the staff can operate. We define a true professional learning community as *a collective of educators who always strive to perform at their ultimate potential, working together to learn, grow, and improve the professional practice of teaching in order to maximize student learning.*

As baseball's New York Yankees have discovered over the past few years, stockpiling superstars, retaining a Hall of Fame manager, and doling out a huge bankroll are no guarantee of success. The Yankees haven't won the World Series since 2000, despite having 29 players participate in the past 7 All-Star Games, keeping super-manager Joe Torre on board through the 2007 season, and writing the biggest checks in the big leagues: over $200 million in payroll per year. Practices that will more likely result in success include working together as a team, identifying common goals, and relying upon each other to achieve those goals, even for teams with average players, a good manager, and a modest payroll. Just ask the Anaheim Angels, Florida Marlins, Chicago White Sox, and St. Louis Cardinals, teams that won the World Series in 2002, 2003, 2005, and 2006. During their championship seasons, none of these clubs had more than four All-Stars on its roster, and all had a budget in the middle or bottom third of Major League Baseball. The managers and coaches of all these championship teams will tell you that their concept of "team" allowed each and every ballplayer to perform at his best, to the great benefit of the entire squad.

Similarly, PLCs offer schools and teacher teams an umbrella-like framework that allows them to operate in unison while cultivating individual skills. The PLC concept encourages cohesion, common discussions, and interdependence. By all accounts, it allows every member of the school community to benefit from the expertise, strengths, and experience of every other member. It is difficult to imagine meaningful school reform and significant positive change in a school that does not count the PLC concept among its structural assets.

Noted experts on collaborative work in schools have written much more extensively and likely more eloquently than we can on the concept. For more detailed explanations of professional learning communities, see *Professional Learning Communities at Work* (DuFour & Eaker, 1998), *Results Now* (Schmoker, 2006), and *Leading Learning Communities: Standards for What Administrators Should Know and Be Able to Do* (National Association of Elementary School Principals, 2008). The strong bonds between colleagues and their effect on individual and collective growth cannot be overstated, but the two other relationships depicted in the relationship triad in Figure 2.1 are just as important.

Alisa's Approach

The concepts and power of teamwork and collaboration became very clear to me when I first assumed the role of literacy coach at Anderson Elementary. I was charged with working with the teachers of kindergarten and 1st and 2nd grades—a knowledgeable yet very diverse collection of educators.

Almost immediately, I became aware of strained relationships within the group. Along with differing personalities and ranges in age and experience, there were stark disparities in teaching styles and classroom environments. Although the teachers met several times a month for a required PLC meeting, they had little awareness of the instruction taking place in their colleagues' classrooms. Lunchtime was a quiet affair. Some teachers gathered in one classroom, others paired up and ate separately, and still others opted to keep to themselves. Grade-pair meetings (at which all K–2 teachers convened) were often filled with tension: on one side, a few loud voices holding the floor; on the other, silent resentment. It was difficult to find trust or respect among the crowd, and positive, professional conversation was hard to come by.

For two years, I tackled the peculiarities of this group of educators with all the tricks I could dig out of my coaching toolbox. We set individual goals, we set team goals, we engaged in book clubs, we observed each other's classrooms, we researched areas of interest together, we analyzed data, we shared students in reading groups—it was an exhausting, demanding, trying time, but in the end it was well worth the efforts and trials, because in the process we had created a truly authentic professional learning community of primary grades teachers. Now, the entire K–2 staff eagerly congregates in one teacher's room three or four times a week for a shared lunchtime conversation. The conversation sometimes drifts to weekend plans or baseball scores, but more often it's a respectful debate (homogeneous grouping versus heterogeneous grouping) or an intense professional discussion (How can we better meet the needs of our English language learners?). And this is in *addition* to the planned weekly meetings and scheduled collaboration times!

A New Frontier: Instructional Coaches

Instructional coaches are one of the latest and hottest trends in education. With many educators heeding emerging research that teacher quality is what counts, they are embracing the idea that an on-site staff developer should be hired to teach the teachers. In the Boston public schools alone, a Whole School Improvement and Instructional Coaching Initiative earned a $7.1 million spot in the district's 2005 budget.

Idealists are having a heyday with this educational innovation, yet the new title is rarely accompanied by a specific job description, a meaningful framework for action, guidance, or targeted training on how to bring about positive change in the lives of adults. As educators, we read research indicating that teacher quality is the most important factor in student achievement, so we simply select a good teacher who has the most knowledge (or more likely, the most seniority) from within the ranks of the staff, promote him or her, and bestow upon the teacher the title of "instructional coach." One minute a classroom teacher; the next, a "teacher educator." We don't have a clear idea what that title means or what the person in the role should be doing specifically, but we charge ahead, trusting (or often just *hoping*) that the person with the title will somehow discover the way. At the Washington State Office of the Superintendent of Public Instruction Annual Conference a few years ago, Elizabeth Duffy shared this story about her appointment as an instructional coach:

> Our building administrator saw a need for an educationally proactive position, rather than a reactive one, but there was no job description—I was in uncharted waters. I brought with me over 30 years of teaching experience, depth of knowledge in educational pedagogy, and a willingness to take risks. I was charged with helping teachers teach more effectively so that students learn more effectively. I had no restrictions and no guidelines, just her confidence in my ability as an instructional leader and the expectation that her investment would pay dividends—a daunting charge, one that both excited and terrified me.

As essential and valuable as an instructional leader can be, and as competent and well-intentioned as most are, the potential is also there for this position to cause more damage than good. Without a clear job description that is understood by administrators, coaches, and teachers alike, instructional coaching can easily become divisive and build more resistance to change, which is just the opposite of what it is intended to do. Later in this chapter and more extensively in Part II, we'll do what we can to address this problem by providing a detailed job description for the instructional coach and offering a solid framework from which to design the work of coaches on staff, be they formal instructional coaches, department chairs, grade-level representatives, site-based staff developers, mentors, or any other teacher-leaders on staff.

The Buck Stops Here: Administrators

Whereas the instructional coach is a relatively new position, the school administrator—whether principal, assistant principal, headmaster, director, coordinator, or another title—is a tried-and-true one. Consider your own experiences as a student and as an educator. Although each of the site administrators you have known and worked with has brought a unique and distinctive approach to the position—because of personality, education, background, talents, interests, and style—they all have worked under virtually identical job descriptions.

Administrators have to engage in two diametrically opposed primary behaviors: leading and managing. As clarified in Marcus Buckingham's wonderful guide *The One Thing You Need to Know* (2005), a great leader must "discover what is universal and capitalize on it" (p. 132), whereas a great manager must "discover what is unique about each person and capitalize on it" (p. 83). This makes sense, but it also makes life in the administrator's office difficult. Doing both, and doing them successfully, is the challenge facing modern principals.

Roles and Responsibilities Within the Partnership

In Part III we will discuss in further detail the actions administrators must take to enact Strength-Based School Improvement, but for now we will embark on a deeper investigation into the roles and responsibilities of the building administrator, especially as compared with those of the instructional coach. This simple fact bears repeating: The administrator and coach are teammates in this venture.

And like teammates in any sport, their roles are sometimes distinct, sometimes quite similar, and sometimes overlapping, but the goal is the same. The graphic organizer in Figure 2.2 identifies the primary characteristics of the instructional coach and the building administrator.

Figure 2.2

Characteristics of the Instructional Coach and the Building Administrator

Instructional Coach	*Building Administrator*
Common Responsibilities	
Develops relationships	
Observes teachers	
Analyzes assessments	
Provides resources	
Mentors/challenges teachers	
Strengthens the community of learners	
Distinct Responsibilities	
Peer	Superior
Not an administrator	IS an administrator
Provides constructive feedback	Provides summative feedback
Models lessons	Evaluates lessons
Overlapping Responsibilities	
Servant leadership	Visible leadership
Collaborative goal setting	Directive goal setting
Provides professional development	Coordinates professional development
Counsels teachers	Directs teachers
Motivation	Inspiration

Driving Forces

So, what do coaches and administrators do? As you well know, these intimidating job descriptions could give a Fortune 500 CEO pause. Because here we want to focus on the aspect of the work that leads to positive change and the maximization of teachers' strengths and potential, we will concentrate only on those behaviors directly related to the goal of building teachers' capacity for success. For example, our discussion of the administrator's role intentionally omits budget work, discipline, data analysis, and test administration, among other important duties.

The coach and administrator share the ultimate goal of *effecting positive change*. The administrator may have sole responsibility for crafting a vision and presenting it to staff, but they both are charged with the monumental and complicated task of making that vision a reality. Three driving forces should guide the behaviors of the administrator and coach at all times: (1) building individual relationships, (2) increasing teacher capacity, and (3) strengthening teams and PLCs. Every task administrators and coaches undertake should reflect back to these three concepts and the desire to succeed at putting them in place.

Common Responsibilities

Coaches and administrators have a lot in common. Both work with a variety of teachers, have a workload that extends well beyond the regular contracted hours, and have an immense amount of responsibility for instigating meaningful change. There are a handful of other key behaviors common to both roles.

Developing relationships. The relationships between teacher and coach and teacher and administrator are perhaps the most important and most sensitive elements of schools striving for improvement. Effective coaches and administrators appreciate the magnitude of these relationships, and both work diligently to establish, nurture, and maintain them. Good relationships are characterized by trust, respect, and understanding, and it takes time to create and strengthen them. Our colleague and friend Derek Cordell poses these relationship questions to coaches and administrators: If you were locked in a broken elevator with a teacher, would you be able to carry on a "regular" conversation, or would it be accompanied by awkward periods of silence and discomfort? What do you know about that teacher as a person? With what depth have you cultivated that interpersonal relationship? Effective coaches and administrators devote a significant amount of time and energy to this end. They know that the *real* work occurs only after they've formed a strong bond with each teacher.

Observing teachers. At many times throughout the week, a classroom teacher should look up to see either the coach or the administrator in the classroom. In fact, teachers should *expect* them to spend some time in their classrooms. Although coaches' and administrators' purposes for conducting an observation may differ (see below), both recognize the value in knowing the teachers' skills, strategies, approaches, demeanor, and personality (among many,

many other attributes) in the classroom. Any coach or administrator worth his or her salt will tell you that, as important as knowing the teacher as a *person* is, it's critical to know the teacher as a *teacher.* Such observation periods, effectively used, provide the observer with a plethora of conversation starters, discussion points, shared experiences, and classroom knowledge that can guide collaborative teacher development.

Analyzing assessment data. Over the years, we have all learned a lot about assessment, and formative assessment in particular. Administrators and coaches pore over assessment data with teachers for a variety of purposes: to identify student strengths, to isolate areas of need, to determine trends, to extract shifts in student understanding, and to highlight effective instructional methods. All of these purposes relate to the same goal of designing and altering instructional delivery in the classroom. This is the crux of the whole idea of assessment *for* learning (Stiggins, 2004b), as opposed to the autopsy-like concept of assessment *of* learning. Effective coaches and administrators are data-savvy; they understand the nuances of formative assessments and how analyzing student work samples, pre-assessments, portfolios, surveys, and performance-based assessments can lead to greater rates of student learning and more precision in teaching approaches.

Providing resources. School-based administrators know how to get things done. Through their connections at the district level, access to budgets, links to departments, and affinity for the bottom line, they have immeasurable resources to provide to teachers. Likewise, instructional coaches offer teachers deep content knowledge and rigorous pedagogical expertise, as well as access to programs, coordinators, and a wealth of other information. In the process of Strength-Based School Improvement, individuals in both positions make their resources available to each and every teacher who could benefit from them. For example, a coach can identify a teacher's need and find a short workshop they might attend together. An administrator can find the budgetary support and put plans in place for collaborative work. Working together, they can ensure that each teacher gets the support and assistance he or she deserves.

Mentoring and challenging teachers. A mentor is like a bridge builder, spanning the chasm between two entities to build a deeper understanding, strengthen the bond, and open communication lines to encourage mutual development

(Hall, 2008a; Janas, 1996). Both administrators and coaches engage in mentoring behaviors—encouraging, nourishing, and motivating—to help individual teachers develop skills and strategies and to enhance professional practice. As we discussed, individuals in both positions have access to a tremendous amount of resources to share with teachers, and savvy coaches and administrators channel a good portion of their energy into challenging teachers to extend their thinking, step beyond their comfort zones, and push themselves toward excellence.

Strengthening the community of learners. We mentioned earlier the importance of PLCs in schools. Administrators have the power and authority to make appropriate modifications to schedules and program designs that will encourage frequent and meaningful collaboration between teachers. Building a community of lifelong learners takes more than common prep times, built-in teacher collaboration time, and shared projects, however; with precise support and intervention from a coach, teams of teachers can establish and meet common goals, analyze assessments together, share in professional learning opportunities, and participate in joint lesson study sessions. And as administrators and coaches talk with teacher teams, ask them questions, encourage self-reflection, and challenge their limits, the teams become stronger and more viable.

Distinct Responsibilities

Despite commonalities, the roles of coach and administrator are distinguished by several notable differences. In order to be effective, both must embrace the characteristics we highlight. It is especially important that the coach stay on the coach's side of these dichotomies. These descriptions, actions, and behaviors are nonnegotiable. A single misstep—either inadvertent straying or intentional infiltration—could threaten the relationship's viability. The teachers trust that coaches and administrators will exhibit these positional behaviors, and nothing ruins relationships quicker than a violation of that trust.

Being a peer versus being a supervisor. When we think of peer relations, we think of people who are of equal rank and work in similar positions. Coaches and teachers meet this definition; they share the same work. Neither wields any power over the other, and neither has to answer to the other. But an administrator holds a position of higher rank and power than the classroom teacher, and both coach and teacher report to the administrator in the same fashion.

Having administrative duties versus having no administrative duties. In a school setting, the site-based staff developer or instructional coach is generally employed by the school district under the same negotiated agreement as teachers. Administrators have separate contracts and are typically members of a distinct bargaining unit. Crossing the line into administrative function is where the majority of trust-violating coaching behaviors occur. When coaches begin to act as administrators (either of their own volition or on an administrator's orders), the leverage they once had in the classroom disappears.

Providing constructive feedback versus providing summative feedback. A coach observing a lesson should provide feedback that is geared entirely toward *making the teaching better*. This is not to say that an administrator's feedback cannot contain much of the same elements; in fact, a great deal of Part III addresses how an administrator can provide constructive feedback to teachers. But instructional coaches do not, cannot, should not, and must not ever provide any sort of summative feedback to teachers. That is the sole responsibility of the evaluative administrator—never the coach. The administrator is the only one whose professional responsibilities include giving summative feedback. At the end of the day, week, semester, or year, the administrator will tell teachers if their work exceeded expectations, was satisfactory, or needed improvement. This is never the coach's task.

Modeling lessons versus evaluating lessons. When visiting a teacher's classroom, coaches and administrators have specific responsibilities and focus points. For example, the coach models lessons to share new instructional strategies, demonstrate a different way to teach, or give the teacher the opportunity to see the coach's new professional learning in action. During this modeling and subsequent discussion, the coach does not make any sort of evaluative judgments; this responsibility is left to the administrator. Since the administrator's primary function is to ensure the smooth operation of the entire educational facility, he or she must evaluate every mechanism within. Naturally, this evaluative attention extends to lessons observed in the classroom. Again, we realize there are times that an administrator can model a lesson for a teacher; however, there is never a time for a coach to evaluate a teacher's classroom instruction.

Overlapping Responsibilities

Sometimes the borders between the positions of coach and administrator are a bit fuzzy. Depending on the situation, the school, the personnel, and the relationships between staff members, either the coach or the administrator could perform one or both of the paired tasks that follow.

Servant leadership/visible leadership. There is much research on the value of servant leadership, a term first coined by Robert Greenleaf in 1970 and still in full swing today. The servant leader is one who puts the needs of others ahead of his or her own and begins to act as a facilitator. A servant leader might say, "What can I do to help you achieve this goal?" Understanding the concept of visible leadership requires a subtle shift in perspective. The visible leader stands ahead of the crowd, acting as a figurehead of sorts and rallying the staff. "Follow me to the promised land," states the visible leader. Either coach or administrator could facilitate teachers' acquisition of new skills behind the scenes, and either could stand in front of a camera and answer a reporter's questions about the recent rise in test scores.

Collaborative goal setting/direct goal setting. Both the coach and administrator play a role in the initial process of establishing goals for individual teachers. Typically, the coach works alongside teachers, asking them what their focus area is, how they came to select that goal, and what support they will need to achieve it. The administrator could do the same thing, but in the case of certain teachers, the conversation could be more pointed. Specifically, the administrator could select the goal for the teacher—perhaps when the administrator has concerns about the teacher's performance or goal-setting focus or when the teacher just needs a little direction. Coaches can engage in similar behaviors but must be significantly more careful practicing directive approaches because of their relationship status as peers.

Providing professional development/coordinating professional development. Throughout the course of events in education, teachers require support, intervention, and extension of their own professional learning. Enter the coach and administrator. Ideally, while both share the load as far as identifying needs and developing plans, the coach handles the lion's share of the professional development actions, through modeling, teaching, discussing, and mentoring. The administrator's participation is generally more behind the scenes, focused on coordinating the registration and funding of workshops, scheduling substitute coverage when necessary, and making logistical arrangements to ensure that teachers' learning needs are met. As you might imagine, the lines are blurry here because either could play a role to some extent in any step along this process.

Counseling teachers/directing teachers. As a peer, a coach is on the same level as the teachers. If the coach is behaving as a coach (and not as an administrator), then it is perfectly within his or her rights to offer—and seek—counsel with teachers on staff. A good deal of counseling consists of listening and offering empathy. Because of the inherent evaluative implication of administrators' work with teachers, it's a stretch to suppose that administrators and teachers can engage in this kind of counseling with any frequency. Administrators are more likely to listen with an ear inclined less toward empathy and more toward solutions. However, relationships between coach and teacher and administrator and teacher vary in depth and strength, meaning the occasions in which coach and administrator can venture into their counterpart roles likewise vary.

Motivating/inspiring. Reflect on the beginning of a school year. When teachers gather together in the freshness of autumn, they may receive an inspirational speech from their administrator designed to set the scene for motivation, strategy, enthusiasm, and confidence. After the fanfare fades and the teachers face the reality that students will be entering their classrooms in a matter of days, instructional coaches continue to foster motivation and enthusiasm by providing unilateral backing and encouragement. Again, relationships dictate whether or not (and to what degree) these lines are blurred as coach, administrator, and teacher strive for individual and collective capacity building.

The Partnership's Results

When the collaborative partnership between the instructional coach and the building administrator is effective, the positive results are clear. The school community benefits from the expansion of the teachers' instructional capacity, and, as a direct consequence, the school makes progress toward its ultimate goal of increased student achievement.

The actions and approaches of the coach and the administrator should complement one another. As we have discussed, there are a few tasks that are apportioned to one or the other—providing a yin to the other's yang—that help keep a healthy balance for teachers. This balance, in fact, strengthens the concept of triangulation, as it provides strong relationships with each teacher from slightly different angles. The key is for the coach and the administrator to view their roles as interdependent, relying on each other to fully support, challenge, and guide teachers as they strive for improvement.

Part II

Coaching Along the Continuum

Reflection is the beginning of reform.

—Mark Twain

Creating a niche for an instructional coach can be a shot in the arm for beleaguered schools and districts seeking to demystify school improvement. Implemented effectively, instructional coaching can facilitate professional learning, instigate growth, strengthen relationships, and unite learning communities. Unfortunately, most coaches receive very little direction and even less role definition, and this imprecision can handicap even the most well-intentioned. In this section, we begin with Chapter 3's introduction to the roles and responsibilities of coaches within our model and then offer a framework for taking meaningful action based on the specific strengths and needs of the teachers with whom the coach will work.

Although we don't pretend there is an exact, foolproof formula to follow, we do think that by understanding some fundamental truths about human behavior and following our Continuum of Self-Reflection (introduced in Chapter 4 and detailed in Chapters 5–8), an instructional coach can build teachers' capacity for success by helping them reflect on their practices and make positive changes in their classrooms that will improve student learning.

We preface this part of the book with a personal word of warning for readers who are instructional coaches: Reading these chapters may challenge your perspective as a coach, a teacher, and a learner. You will be asked to set aside any feelings of pride or power in your position. You will be asked to evaluate your personal openness to learning new things. You will be challenged to dispose of preconceived notions of staff members and asked to look for strengths and hidden potential among the most difficult and challenging of colleagues. All of this requires profound, thoughtful reflection as a coach.

The relationships between coaches and individual teachers are critical, as is the notion of teamwork and collaboration among staff. And although instructional coaches could read and reread this section all by itself as a way to hone their own craft and influence, ideally the information found here will complement and support the work of the building administrator. This is the critical partnership, as coach and administrator pursue their goals in tandem.

3

Introduction to the Coach's Role

For the instructional coach, piecing together a job description gives rise to many questions: Where do I begin? What's the ultimate goal of my work? How do I structure my time? When do I get into classrooms? How do I connect with challenging staff members? What do I do if a colleague is resistant? And, most important, how do I get teachers to *want* to make positive changes within their classrooms?

Instructional coaches begin by looking at themselves. As was said so eloquently by Richard Henry Dunn, "He who dares to teach must never cease to learn" (Fiore & Whitaker, 2005, p. 148).

What Makes an Effective Coach?

Just as an impressive résumé does not ensure an employee's effectiveness, experience, content knowledge, and teaching skill do not guarantee success in a coaching position. Individuals seeking to thrive in this realm must possess and cultivate a slew of other interpersonal and professional skills. Let's take a few moments to look at the characteristics of an effective coach.

An effective coach is highly self-reflective. You can't teach others what you don't first embrace yourself. John Dewey defined *reflection* as "turning a subject over in the mind and giving it serious consecutive consideration. It enables us to act in a deliberate and intentional fashion" (1933, p. 3). The ability to ruminate and to critically analyze your own performance and personal attitudes cannot be overstated. The most effective coach will not have all the answers, but his or her inquiry-approach to learning, awareness of personal strengths and weaknesses, and desire to grow professionally will be evident to all. Self-reflection is at the heart of all he or she does.

An effective coach is able to build and maintain trustworthy relationships. Think of the last time someone convinced you to make a significant change in your life. Maybe it was giving up smoking, taking up exercising, or even changing religions. Who was the person who helped to persuade you? Most likely, it was a person you are very close with—someone you respect and trust. Effective coaches have strong interpersonal and people skills. They realize the importance of connecting, cultivating, nurturing, and developing relationships. They understand that a teacher is much more likely to take part in a learning venture with someone he or she trusts. They also understand that a teacher is much more likely to resist being asked to change by someone with whom he or she has no connection.

An effective coach is skilled in recognizing others' strengths, abilities, and beliefs. It is becoming clearer and clearer to us that "successful people, in any field, work out of their strengths, not their weaknesses" (Kise, 2006, p. 12).

The prevalent mind-set in today's world is that we must identify our weaknesses and work to improve them in order to better ourselves. Collectively, we seem to hold the belief that an individual's greatest capacity for growth is found in his or her weaknesses, but that perception couldn't be further from the truth. Our strengths are what drive us; they propel us to do what we do. For coaches, effectiveness comes from recognizing and helping to refine an individual's strengths and talents, seeing potential where others see shortcomings.

An effective coach is a servant leader. For servant leaders, true power in leadership does not come from the ability to dictate or command; rather, it comes from having a clear vision and the desire and wisdom to guide others toward a common goal. Greenleaf (1970) defines the role as "one who seeks to draw out, inspire, and develop the best and highest within people from the inside out" (p. 3). He goes on to say, "Leadership becomes an interdependent work rather than an immature interplay between strong, independent, ego-driven rulers and compliant dependent followers" (p. 11). Effective coaches should think of themselves as servant first: supporting teachers behind the scenes and seeking to make everyone else an expert rather than touting themselves as the only source of expertise. This attitude is key to coaching success.

An effective coach is patient. Genuine change doesn't occur overnight; it is gradual and deliberate. Effective coaches recognize slight improvements and notice the "baby steps" that teachers make, but they also recognize that change is difficult and sometimes tedious work. To truly change, one must invest a great deal of time. Coaches who walk alongside teachers and share in the incremental successes will find that success really does beget further success.

An effective coach considers "the bus question." Imagine that on the way home from work tomorrow, you, an instructional coach, are hit by a bus. Facing a long recovery period and unable to return to the job for a long time, one question looms large in your mind: How are teachers better off for having worked with you? Has your coaching helped them to embrace meaningful change, build their capacity, increase their instructional skill, and strengthen their self-reflective tendencies? Have you acted merely as a stop-gap, covering up their weaknesses, or has your work built upon their strengths and helped to create better learning environments for their students? Effective coaches answer affirmatively and can provide reams of data and anecdotal evidence to support this claim.

Pete's Perspective

As a principal, I have worked with a variety of instructional coaches. Each one has operated under a slightly different title (some of which I made up), but they have all been responsible for working alongside, in front of, and slightly behind the instructional staff in my schools. Some of the coaches were incredibly effective, garnering impressive levels of individual and collective professional development and increased student achievement. Others floundered and left us all scratching our heads. What was the difference?

Quite simply, the difference was in their people skills. I realize this characteristic is difficult to quantify, but anyone who has ever interacted with another human being knows exactly what I'm referring to. People skills are the common thread that weaves together the six characteristics of an effective coach . . . those undeniable elements of someone's personality that can determine whether we laugh or grimace, invite or shun, grow or wither. When the time comes to hire a coach, rummage through the top candidates' figurative closets to ensure that their personality traits and people skills match your school's needs. A good deal of your future success hangs on that decision.

Relationships, Relationships, Relationships

A recent study conducted at the Kansas University Center for Research on Learning found that within six weeks of starting a new school year, 85 percent of teachers who worked with instructional coaches implemented at least one new instructional strategy (Knight, 2004). By contrast, a separate study on traditional inservice programs (one-shot workshops or presentations) revealed a dismal 10 percent implementation rate (Showers, Murphy, & Joyce, 1996). Clearly, it's worth repeating: "No significant learning occurs without a significant relationship" (Comer, 1995).

Not only do coaches need to be as skilled as classroom teachers and have a vast repertoire of scientifically proven practices to share, but they must also be able to initiate and maintain personal relationships. This includes identifying individuals' strengths and limitations, degree and elements of motivation, work ethic, beliefs, interests, vision, educational background, formative experiences, and professional goals (Kise, 2006). Each of these factors really does play a significant role in the education occurring daily in that teacher's classroom—a larger role, possibly, than that of the curriculum.

Before a coach jumps into the Continuum of Self-Reflection framework, which we'll formally introduce in the next chapter, he or she must first build rapport with each member on staff. Without a solid relationship in place, it's unrealistic to expect the strategies articulated in the Continuum to lead to significant gains. Margaret Wheatley, author of *Leadership and the New Science*, shares this insight: "In organizations, real power and energy is generated through relationships. The patterns of relationships and the capacities to form them are more important than tasks, functions, roles, and positions" (Secretan, 2004, p. 27).

So, as a coach, how do you begin? You begin by spending as much time as you can with teachers, getting to know them and allowing them to get to know you. Volunteering to help is a great place to start. You might offer to work in a teacher's classroom for a short time each day or to help with making copies, putting up a bulletin board, or other odd jobs. Ask teachers to join you for coffee or for a walk during lunch. Instead of putting handouts in teachers' mailboxes, deliver them personally, with a smile. Make it your goal to get into every classroom at least twice a week, and when you're there, look for opportunities to do the following:

- Identify and acknowledge the teacher's individual strengths.
- Validate the teacher's good ideas and ways of doing things.
- Recognize the teacher's areas of talent or personal interest, and connect them to your own.
- Ask questions to engage the teacher on a personal and professional level.

Remember that teachers need to feel comfortable enough with you to be honest, show their weaknesses, and become vulnerable. There must be enough mutual trust and respect that the teacher will respond to being asked to change at such a personal level. The authors of *Issues in Mentoring* state, "Mentoring demands befriending. While it is difficult to delineate all of the behaviors associated with befriending, two critical ones stand out: accepting and relating" (Kerry & Mayes, 1995, p. 31).

When a teacher and a coach can enter into a collaborative relationship with the expressed goal of learning together, the results are advantageous to all. Not only do both teacher and coach enhance their professional skills, but by working together, they also engage in the practice of reflection. Ultimately, the students reap the benefits. It's a win-win-win situation.

Self-Reflection

Not all change is good. We recognize that, so the question becomes this: How do you teach teachers to resist the "bad" changes and seek out the "good" ones? The answer lies in a simple yet profound concept: self-reflection. It's not the *doing* that matters, said revered educator John Dewey, "it's the *thinking* about the doing" (quoted in Archambault, 1974, p. 321, emphasis added). Whether the teacher is a leading expert on best practices or a new educator who knows very little about how to run a classroom, what matters most is the teacher's personal level of self-reflection. In fact, we believe that a teacher's ability to self-reflect is directly linked to his or her classroom effectiveness. Self-reflection, therefore, is a fundamental component building a teacher's capacity for success.

Daudelin and Hall (1997) describe reflective learning as "the process of stepping back from an experience to ponder carefully and persistently its meaning . . . to reflect on the learning that is occurring" (p. 13). The coaching framework we propose through the Strength-Based School Improvement model is based on the idea that individuals who are self-reflective will exhibit these characteristics:

- They will think about their thinking (Dewey, 1933; Schön, 1983).
- They will have an increased awareness of personal strengths and weaknesses, becoming more effective and efficient as professionals (Dewey, 1933; Kolb, 1984).
- They will be increasingly intentional in their instruction—know what they are doing and why they are doing it (Perry, 1998; Schön, 1983).
- They will demonstrate more sensitivity to how their instruction affects their students (McCarthy, 1996; Schön, 1983; Wolcott & Lynch, 1997).
- They will be more open to mandated changes from within their building, district, and state (Dewey, 1933; Furlong & Maynard, 1995).
- They will be more collaborative and actively participate in professional learning communities (Eyler, Giles, & Schmeide, 1996; Guskin, 1994).
- They will be intrinsically motivated to continue learning and empowered to seek new ways to better themselves (Dewey, 1933; Kolb, 1984).

The skill of self-reflection transcends all other skills, strategies, and teaching approaches because it can grow over the course of a teacher's career and enable the teacher to cultivate and solidify all of his or her professional learning. In *Systems for Change in Literacy Education*, master educators Carol A. Lyons and Gay Su Pinnell point out, "You do not learn to be a good teacher of reading and writing in a few months, in a year, or even over a period of several years. Teaching skills develop over a lifetime" (2001, p. ix). This is the impact an effective instructional coach can make when he or she can guides teachers in a proper direction using a feasible framework: the Continuum of Self-Reflection.

4

The Coaching Framework

In *It's About Learning (and It's About Time)*, Stoll, Fink, and Earl (2003) quote Stephanie Hirsch, executive director of the National Staff Development Council:

> For teachers, going to school must be as much about learning as it is about teaching. They must have time each day to learn, plan lessons, critique student work, and support improvement as members of learning teams. . . . Staff development cannot be something educators do only on specified days in the school calendar. It must be part of every educator's daily work schedule. (p. 98)

This is where your role as an instructional coach comes into play. The pursuit of knowledge is a conscious, deliberate, and collaborative effort. The adult learners you are working with are a diverse collection of educators who espouse different beliefs, offer different perspectives, and work with different intensities toward the common goal of student achievement. How do you make sense of all that you learn about each individual? How do you build collaborative relationships around the pursuit of knowledge? We recommend you begin by using the Continuum of Self-Reflection.

What Is the Continuum of Self-Reflection?

Figure 4.1 shows the Continuum at a glance: four developmental stages through which teachers generally progress as they become skilled in the art of self-reflection. As the more detailed overview in Figure 4.2 illustrates, these phases denote gains in expertise, experience, motivation, knowledge, and most definitively, self-reflective abilities. Identifying what stage a teacher is in helps a coach determine that teacher's specific learning needs and create a successful coaching plan, built on the strategies outlined in the Continuum. This precise approach to on-site, embedded staff development can yield tremendous benefits as teachers become more aware, more confident, better motivated, more knowledgeable, and increasingly self-reflective.

When we refer to the stages of the Continuum of Self-Reflection, what we're talking about are states of mind, levels of self-awareness, and phases in the self-reflective process. We've chosen the term "stage" to emphasize that self-reflection is a progressive process. We do *not* mean to suggest a categorical definition of an individual's development. In fact, a teacher may demonstrate characteristics of more than one stage simultaneously and be in different stages while teaching different subjects or courses, for example. Our intent is for you to view the teacher characteristics and classroom characteristics associated with each stage more as reference points than as a comprehensive list of behaviors and attributes to be "checked off" before the teacher can "advance" to the next stage. Essentially, the Continuum is a tool to help school leaders understand a teacher's current state of mind and identify the approaches that will encourage deeper reflective habits.

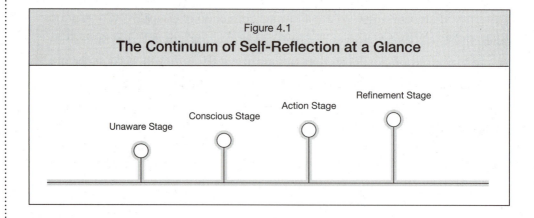

Figure 4.1

The Continuum of Self-Reflection at a Glance

Unaware Stage

Conscious Stage

Action Stage

Refinement Stage

Figure 4.2
The Continuum of Self-Reflection: Coach's Model

	Teacher's Reflective Tendencies	Related Classroom Characteristics	Your Role as Coach	Coaching Strategies That Foster Reflective Growth
Unaware Stage	• Demonstrates little or no awareness of instructional reality in the classroom • Focuses on routine • Exhibits the best of intentions • Expresses confusion about own role in learning • Collaborates with colleagues on a superficial level • Defines problems inaccurately • Focuses on the job itself—the *act* of teaching	• Scripted lessons, with little or no teacher modeling • Passive learning, with little or no student interaction • Lessons built on direct instruction and assignments • Little or no evidence of systematic, standards-based planning • No differentiation of instruction • Little or no awareness of effective time management • No link between instruction and assessment • Little effort to make curriculum relevant to students	*Unconditional Partner* • Identify strengths, limitations, and needs • Recognize potential • Build trust through interpersonal relationships • Share your personal experience of becoming aware of different instructional strategies • Create a collaborative environment	• Visit the classroom • Seek additional opportunities to build rapport • Identify a specific instructional problem to build awareness around • Use specific questioning to establish rationales for teaching practices • Administer personal belief and reflective questionnaires • Provide opportunities to observe in other classrooms • Advocate journal keeping • Facilitate opportunities to exchange ideas with others during guided meetings

Capacity-Building Goal: *To create awareness of the need for change and foster a desire to learn*

	Teacher's Reflective Tendencies	Related Classroom Characteristics	Your Role as Coach	Coaching Strategies That Foster Reflective Growth
Conscious Stage	• Demonstrates a consistent "knowing–doing" gap • Can ambiguously cite research to support current teaching methods • Makes excuses for problems • Demonstrates limited ability to evaluate problems • Becomes easily distracted from goals • Collaborates inconsistently with colleagues • Disregards others' ideas • Focuses first on self	• Instruction designed for teacher convenience • Short-term planning evident yet inconsistent • Occasional links between instruction and assessment • Little student engagement in active, meaningful learning • Little problem solving from students • Occasional differentiation of instruction • Noticeable swings in instructional approaches	*Motivator and Strategist* • Praise generously • Reach out to include teacher in collaborative work • Communicate and maintain a clear vision • Build confidence through short-term goal setting • Focus on small changes • Make daily contact, checking in often to talk about goals and progress toward them	• Provide daily feedback highlighting instructional strengths • Examine and discuss student data • Develop a detailed action plan • Focus on short-term, attainable goals that will have long-term impact • Provide support for instructional goals and best-practice strategies • Meet weekly for collaborative lesson planning (guided planning) • Model specific techniques and provide ample time for discussion • Design meetings around a specific instructional topic

Capacity-Building Goal: *To motivate and show how to apply pedagogical knowledge consistently*

Figure 4.2—*(continued)*
The Continuum of Self-Reflection: Coach's Model

	Teacher's Reflective Tendencies	Related Classroom Characteristics	Your Role as Coach	Coaching Strategies That Foster Reflective Growth
Action Stage	• Accepts responsibility for the success of all students and for own personal growth • Evaluates issues and situations objectively • Seeks to incorporate research-based concepts and strategies • Reflects upon teaching only after the action • Believes in only one "right" way of doing things • Struggles to identify solutions to long-term problems • Receives feedback well, then enters a critical loop • Collaborates on a limited basis with colleagues • Focuses on the *science* of teaching	• Regular use of assessment to monitor student progress • Consistent application of best-practice instructional strategies • Lessons linked to standards • Evidence of limited long-term planning • Classroom appears functional, but gaps are lurking	*Mentor* • Validate ideas, actions, and instructional decisions • Release responsibility and encourage independence • Provide research from which to construct meaning • Model open-mindedness toward multiple approaches and perspectives • Collaboratively engage in diagnosis and action planning	• Invite participation in small-group discussions • Use the Apprenticeship Model • Use classroom observation with specific feedback • Videotape and analyze performance together • Foster idea-sharing through collegial observations • Use reflective questioning • Create a dialogue journal • Encourage participation in a professional book club • Encourage workshop attendance as a way to share learning • Analyze individual student data together • Publicly recognize expertise • Help develop a system for storing and organizing information

Capacity-Building Goal: *To build on experience and help strengthen expertise*

	Teacher's Reflective Tendencies	Related Classroom Characteristics	Your Role as Coach	Coaching Strategies That Foster Reflective Growth
Refinement Stage	• Reflects before, during, and after taking action • Recognizes that there are multiple "right" courses of action • Maintains a vast repertoire of instructional strategies • Engages in action research as common practice • Modifies lessons and plans to meet students' needs • Pursues opportunities to work and learn with colleagues • Thinks beyond the classroom • Focuses on the *art* of teaching	• Assessment drives daily instruction • Students largely responsible for their own learning • Multiple instructional strategies in use	*Collaborator* • Compliment creativity and originality • Bring attention to hard work • Stimulate discussions of personal vision and educational philosophy • Practice "mirror-listening" • Ask questions to drive personal reflection and growth	• Provide a wide range of pedagogical resources • Encourage book club facilitation or initiation • Analyze group data together • Establish a team action research project • Encourage conference participation and publication submission • Arrange for student-teacher hosting opportunities • Promote talent development • Encourage leadership

Capacity-Building Goal: *To encourage long-term growth and continued reflection*

Teachers in the Unaware Stage

Teachers in this first stage of the Continuum of Self-Reflection have no awareness that their classroom could be any different than it currently is. They have little or no knowledge of research-based instructional practices and a limited understanding of their own role in student learning. They may be some of the hardest-working individuals on staff, yet they consistently yield the smallest gains in student achievement.

Our goal is to increase awareness of the need for change and foster a desire to learn. Unaware teachers will be more likely to see the importance of change if the coach can build connections between problems that arise in the classroom and evidence-based instructional strategies. Often mistakenly assumed to be unwilling to learn, teachers in the Unaware stage tend to accept without question the world in which they teach. They need an unconditional partner to help them look beyond the routine of what they do each day and realize the impact that they could have.

Teachers in the Conscious Stage

In this second stage on the Continuum, there is a disconnect between teachers' knowledge of best practices and daily classroom instruction. Conscious-stage teachers are aware of what they *should* be doing and often contemplate or attempt a new strategy, but they lack the motivation and consistency to apply their knowledge in a meaningful way. They often choose to do what is best, easiest, or most convenient for themselves over what is best for their students.

Our goal is to motivate and help them apply pedagogical knowledge more consistently. Teachers in the Conscious stage have very specific needs and require explicit guidance and coaching to address those needs. The coach acts as a motivator and strategist to set specific, short-term goals and to provide support and encouragement to follow through.

Teachers in the Action Stage

When teachers enter the Action stage of the Continuum, they are motivated to change and begin to consistently integrate their knowledge with classroom instruction. They are on a mission to unearth the "right" way to teach, believing that there is one instructional strategy that is better than the rest. They have accepted responsibility for the success of their students and have a beginning recognition of individual needs, even if they lack the knowledge to address those needs in an effective manner. They welcome constructive feedback and openly seek advice.

Our goal is to build on experience and strengthen expertise. The coach will spend the majority of time with Action-stage teachers helping them to build and refine a vast repertoire of instructional strategies. Action teachers want to become experts and will work hard to develop their skills. They have a tendency, though, to view instructional methods as either "right" or "wrong." The coach must work to counteract this natural inclination and to build an awareness of multiple "right" approaches to the same problem.

Teachers in the Refinement Stage

Teachers in the Refinement stage are competent in the art of teaching. They recognize that there may be more than one "right" way of doing things and that their current way of thinking will continue to shift as they engage in reflective learning. They plan and implement strategies that actively engage and support students, making deliberate attempts to allow for multiple ways of learning. Formal and informal assessments, both formative and summative, drive the instruction in their classrooms. They are able to modify and refine plans at a moment's notice in response to student need, interest, and motivation.

Our goal is to encourage long-term growth and continued reflection. The coach should provide a wide range of resources from which Refinement-stage teachers can draw ideas. These teachers are at their best in classrooms where they can be innovative and creative. Although it may seem that teachers in this stage do not need support and assistance, they can always expand on their learning. Rather than providing suggestions during coaching, the coach can guide Refinement teachers' self-reflection and analysis of instructional strategies through open-ended questions and challenges to support all decisions with evidence.

Pete's Perspective

I clearly remember the day Alisa burst into my office, a whirling dervish of energy with ideas exploding from her like an educated Tasmanian devil, talking nineteen to the dozen about reflection, teaching, feedback, and coaching. It was difficult to discern one word from another, but I'm quite sure I nodded and said, "Go for it," which was my standard response to her proposals. She had, and continues to have, a remarkable track record for realizing success.

This time, Alisa was proposing the creation of this coaching model and the Continuum of Self-Reflection, based on the idea that a teacher's accuracy in self-reflective abilities is a fairly accurate precursor to classroom effectiveness. In fact, she declared, the correlation she observed was nothing less than startling.

Over the next few months, Alisa and I researched the concepts of self-reflection, teaching effectiveness, professional development, coaching models, individual strengths, human behavior, and professional relationships. The results of our queries, investigations, observations, and readings reinforced the hypothesis: Self-reflection—in particular, *accurate* and *consistent* self-reflection—proved to be a powerful determinant of teacher (and, by extension, school and student) success.

A Three-Step Coaching Model

Our coaching model consists of a simple series of steps to take with each individual teacher. If you use the Continuum of Self-Reflection, view each teacher as a unique and special human being, and follow these steps, you can further the teachers you work with in their development as professionals and as practitioners of self-reflection, helping them to maximize their potential.

Step One: Meet and Set a Collaborative Professional Growth Goal

The first step of the coaching model is to meet with each teacher one on one and set a collaborative professional growth goal. In her book *The Literacy Coach's Survival Guide*, Cathy Toll reasons that because the process of reflection and change ultimately falls on the individual teacher, "it makes sense that some aspects of literacy coaching might best be done on a one-on-one basis. . . . If a literacy coach wants to help a teacher, the literacy coach needs to include individual conferencing as one of his or her practices" (2005, p. 74).

While there are countless ways to enact this step of the model, a suggested target is to generate one goal with each teacher every quarter. The purposes for setting a collaborative goal are clear:

- It provides a specific focus for the coach's and teacher's work together.
- It holds the coach accountable to both the teacher and the administrator.
- It holds the teacher accountable to both the coach and the administrator.

That being said, let's get real. You may be working in several schools, coaching 65 different teachers in multiple subject areas. You may be working with a teacher (or seven) who won't even smile at you in the hall. In cases like these, meeting one on one with every teacher may not be a reasonable goal. Regardless of the scenario in your building, as a coach you want to have an individual goal for each teacher you are working with, whether it is collaboratively set (the ideal case) or made by you alone (not the best-case scenario but better than no goal at all).

Here are some alternate approaches that can be implemented under less-than-ideal circumstances:

- Identify a schoolwide goal.
- Collaboratively set a grade-level or subject-area goal instead of an individual goal.
- Create a goal for a student or group of students in the teacher's class.
- Identify a project instead of a goal (e.g., write standards as "I can" statements to post in the teacher's classroom).

As you sit down with teachers to set a professional growth goal, walk them through the self-reflection process. Use the Coaching Plan Worksheet (see Figure 4.3) along with the following questions to guide teachers in creating a collaborative goal:

- What type of lessons do you enjoy teaching the most? The least? Why?
- During your lessons, which students are engaged?

	Figure 4.3 — Coaching Plan Worksheet	DOWNLOAD

QTR	What's Going Well	Biggest Challenge
(circle) 1 2 3 4		
	Description of Students Who Are Engaged	**Description of Students Who Are Unengaged**
	Instructional Focus	**Collaborative Goal**
	Teacher's Role	**Coach's Role**
	☐ Try new strategy ☐ Refine existing strategy ☐ Read article/book ☐ Set lesson/planning goal ☐ Observe coach ☐ Observe colleague ☐ View videotape ☐ Keep reflective journal ☐ Reorganize _____ ☐ Other:	☐ Supply information (evidence or examples) ☐ Access resources ☐ Aid lesson planning/Help prioritize lesson elements ☐ Model/Demonstrate ☐ Observe and give feedback ☐ Facilitate collegial observation ☐ Analyze assessments ☐ Other:
	Plan	**Evidence of Success**
	Goal Met? ☐ Yes ☐ No	

• Which students do you have difficulty reaching? Which of your students are unengaged?

• Do you have a particular subject area that you would like to make the focus of this quarter's collaborative goal?

• How can I support you in this professional goal this quarter?

Finally, there's this question, courtesy of Cathy Toll (2005): "When you think about your goals for teaching—the kind of readers and writers you want your students to be, the kind of classroom you want to have, and the kind of work you want to do—what gets in your way?" (p. 59).

Step Two: Create an Individualized Coaching Plan

An expert classroom teacher assesses each student before planning instruction. In the same way, instructional coaches should begin the year informally assessing the adult learners they are working with using the Continuum of Self-Reflection. The collaborative goal-setting meeting is an excellent place to collect this valuable information.

After setting a professional development goal with each teacher, take a moment to sit down and determine the teacher's present stage on the Continuum of Self-Reflection. Using information from the Coaching Plan Worksheet, record teachers' names on the Coach's Goal List by Continuum Stage found in Figure 4.4 (pp. 50–51).

Once you've got the form set up, consider the similarities of the classrooms of the teachers in each group. Look at the goals and use the following questions to guide the creation of each teacher's individualized coaching plan:

1. What role do I need to play in this teacher's life this quarter?

2. How can I accomplish this work?

3. Can I find similarities in individual goals so that I can arrange for teachers to work collaboratively?

4. Looking at this teacher's goal, can I find other teachers on staff who are strong in this area?

5. How can I get this teacher into colleagues' classrooms so that they can learn from one another?

6. What specific strategies from the Continuum of Self-Reflection will help me guide the teacher toward his or her goal?

7. How often does this teacher need to see me: daily, weekly, biweekly? What are the needs of other teachers in this stage?

With the answers to these questions in mind, you should have a fairly good picture of what your job is going to look like. It's now time to pull out your calendar. Continually review the Coaching Plan Worksheet, the Coach's Goal List, and the questions above and create a series of quarterly, monthly, and weekly coaching plans.

Step Three: Implement, Document, and Reflect

As you identify stages on the Continuum of Self-Reflection and create your coaching plan, it is important to remember that this is not an exercise in labeling groups of teachers into static categories, such as "key members" and "deadwood" (Evans, 2001) or "thoroughbreds" and "ain't cuttin' its" (Hall, 2004). Rather, this is an investigation into the driving forces, self-reflective concepts, and professional expertise of individual human beings. It is work that demands a fluid set of descriptions—and initial notes in pencil.

While implementing your plan, keep anecdotal notes of teacher interactions and progress made. You may feel the need to document each time that you go into a classroom or work with a teacher. When you meet again at the beginning of the following quarter, you should have plenty of evidence showing how you have provided support toward the collaborative goal. This is also an appropriate time to consider and reflect upon your effectiveness as a coach. You may be able to measure your impact by the amount of growth demonstrated by the teacher, and with sufficient documentation, you can attribute certain portions of that growth to specific coaching behaviors.

Understanding Human Behavior

You've worked hard to build relationships, identify the stages that teachers are in, and create specific coaching plans. Now you are ready to push teachers to begin to make a positive change. All of a sudden, some teachers may show signs of unwillingness. What gives? In her book *Differentiated Coaching*, Jane Kise tells

Figure 4.4

Coach's Goal List by Continuum Stage

DOWNLOAD

Quarter (circle one): 1 2 3 4

Teacher	Quarterly Goal	Your Role as Coach	Coaching Strategies That Foster Growth
Unaware Stage		*Unconditional Partner* • Identify strengths, limitations, and needs • Recognize potential • Build trust through interpersonal relationships • Share your personal experience of becoming aware of different instructional strategies • Create a collaborative environment	• Visit the classroom • Seek additional opportunities to build rapport • Identify a specific instructional problem to build awareness around • Use specific questioning to establish rationales for teaching practices • Administer personal belief and reflective questionnaires • Provide opportunities to observe in other classrooms • Advocate journal keeping • Facilitate opportunities to exchange ideas with others during guided meetings

Capacity-Building Goal: *To create awareness of the need for change and foster a desire to learn*

Teacher	Quarterly Goal	Your Role as Coach	Coaching Strategies That Foster Growth
Conscious Stage		*Motivator and Strategist* • Praise generously • Reach out to include teacher in collaborative work • Communicate and maintain a clear vision • Build confidence through short-term goal setting • Focus on small changes • Make daily contact, checking in often to talk about goals and progress toward them	• Provide daily feedback highlighting instructional strengths • Examine and discuss student data • Develop a detailed action plan • Focus on short-term, attainable goals that will have long-term impact • Provide support for instructional goals and best-practice strategies • Meet weekly for collaborative lesson planning (guided planning) • Model specific techniques and provide ample time for discussion • Design meetings around a specific instructional topic

Capacity-Building Goal: *To motivate and show how to apply pedagogical knowledge consistently*

Quarter (circle one): 1   2   3   4

Teacher	Quarterly Goal	Your Role as Coach	Coaching Strategies That Foster Growth
		Mentor • Validate ideas, actions, and instructional decisions • Release responsibility and encourage independence • Provide research from which to construct meaning • Model open-mindedness toward multiple approaches and perspectives • Collaboratively engage in diagnosis and action planning	• Invite participation in small-group discussions • Use the Apprenticeship Model • Use classroom observation and provide specific feedback • Videotape and analyze performance together • Foster idea sharing through collegial observations • Use reflective questioning • Create a dialogue journal • Encourage participation in a professional book club • Encourage workshop attendance as a way to share learning • Analyze individual student data together • Publicly recognize expertise • Help develop a system for storing and organizing information

Action Stage

Capacity-Building Goal: *To build on experience and help strengthen expertise*

| | | *Collaborator*
• Compliment creativity and originality
• Bring attention to hard work
• Stimulate discussions of personal vision and educational philosophy
• Practice "mirror-listening"
• Ask questions to drive personal reflection and growth | • Provide a wide range of pedagogical resources
• Encourage book club facilitation or initiation
• Analyze group data together
• Establish a team action research project
• Encourage conference participation and publication submission
• Arrange for student-teacher hosting opportunities
• Promote talent development
• Encourage leadership |

Refinement Stage

Capacity-Building Goal: *To encourage long-term growth and continued reflection*

us, "Change is hard work, even when we want to change and are convinced it's worth the effort" (2006, p. 4).

The fact is, no matter who you are and no matter how skilled you are, if your job is working closely with other adults and guiding them to try new things, you will encounter some degree of defensiveness, whether it comes in the form of initial reluctance or hits with full-blown emotional defiance. An effective coach anticipates and is prepared for such reactions, for it is at these crucial moments that everything you've worked toward—every positive step you've taken—can suddenly disappear. There are three essentials to keep in mind:

• When people feel vulnerable or threatened, they often get defensive or reactive (Coons, 2005).

• In this state, their listening begins to shut down (Wood, 2005).

• It is important to stay neutral, be empathetic, and assess their state of mind before responding (Osterman & Kottkamp, 2004).

There are volumes of literature dedicated to identifying why people resist change. Rick Maurer (2007) identifies three simple levels of resistance that can help us understand the potential reasons behind negative response to new ways of doing things (see Figure 4.5). When you meet resistance, stop and reflect about the reasons behind the behavior. Once you have identified likely motives, return to the Continuum of Self-Reflection and alter your approach with the teacher. By attempting to address the real reason behind the unwelcoming response, you can likely pull the person out of a negative state into a more positive one, ultimately guiding him or her further down the path of self-reflection.

This Is Doable

Instructional coaches are nominally meant to help Mrs. Ramburado begin to differentiate reading instruction or help Mr. Dyer with classroom management. But what if, while we do that, we are also able to guide those teachers in the deeper art of self-reflection? Mrs. Ramburado won't always have a coach by her side to identify differentiation strategies, and Mr. Dyer won't always have a second adult in the room to attempt de-escalation strategies. Fostering self-reflection encourages individual development and growth, going beyond quick solutions to today's challenges.

Figure 4.5

Levels of Resistance and Possible Explanations

Level 1: "I Don't Get It" (Reluctance)

1. *Ambiguity.* The reason for the change is unclear.

2. *Poor communication.* The teacher doesn't understand why the change is necessary.

3. *Disagreement with data.* The teacher doesn't believe the change will work.

   • There may be evidence that the old way works.

   • There is little or no evidence that the new way will work.

   • There is confusion over what the data mean.

4. *Poor timing.* The teacher is not ready to hear your suggestion.

   • There are too many things on the teacher's plate right now.

   • There may be personal issues you are unaware of.

Level 2: "I Don't Like It" (Resistance)

1. *Fear of failure.* The teacher is afraid that an attempt to change will be unsuccessful.

2. *Fear of the unknown.* The old way is more comforting.

3. *Fear of personal inadequacy.* The teacher believes that he or she won't be able to build the skills needed.

4. *Excessive pressure.* There is too much pressure from leader or peers to accept the change.

5. *Too much work.* The teacher perceives little or no reward for changing.

6. *Lack of ownership.* The teacher is not involved in the planning.

Level 3: "I Don't Like You" (Defiance)

1. *Climate of mistrust.* The teacher does not trust the motives of the change agent.

2. *Lack of respect.* The teacher does not have a high opinion of those behind the change.

3. *Personality conflict.* The teacher feels that he or she cannot get along socially with those associated with the change.

4. *Unfairness.* The teacher feels as if the situation is somehow unfair.

In the next four chapters, we will delve more deeply into each of the stages of the Continuum, focusing on how to use it as a diagnostic tool in order to engage in intentional coaching approaches. We will provide the typical hallmarks of teachers and classroom practices in each stage, offer suggestions for coaching practices, present some detailed strategies to overcome the inevitable challenges, and give examples of situations in which these plans have worked. So read on, reflect, and prepare to see the benefits of truly effective collaborative coaching.

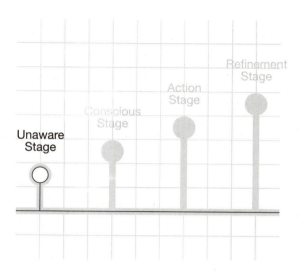

5

The Unaware Stage

We've all been there. We've purchased a new computer, cell phone, iPod, or Blackberry and have become comfortable using it. We know how to check e-mail, download music, and pay bills online. Then someone comes along and asks if they can show us how to use our device in a way that might save us some time or effort. Our first response? Thanks but no thanks! The way we are doing things works for us just fine.

At one time or another, we've all been in the Unaware stage on the Continuum of Self-Reflection: comfortable in the way we do things, unaware of better alternatives, and seeing no need to change. It's as Kruger and Dunning (1999) note in "Unskilled and Unaware of It":

> When people are incompetent in the strategies they adopt to achieve success and satisfaction, they suffer a dual burden: Not only do they reach erroneous conclusions and make unfortunate choices, but their incompetence robs them of the ability to realize it. Instead . . . they are left with the mistaken impression that they are doing just fine. (p. 1121)

Teachers in the Unaware stage exhibit common characteristics both personally and in their classroom. This chapter delves into the role an instructional coach should play with these teachers and provides specific strategies and

5

examples that you can use to shepherd further growth on the Continuum of Self-Reflection. Remember that your primary goal as a coach is not to turn "bad" teachers into "good" teachers, but to empower teachers through the art of self-reflection. Once they have experienced the intrinsic rewards that self-reflection brings, they will naturally be driven to strive for excellence . . . and you may have to look for a new job!

Meet the Teachers

Let's begin now by walking through a couple of classrooms together and taking a closer look at teachers in the Unaware stage.

It's an organized classroom. The desks are in neat rows, and the students are quiet and on task. A 10-year veteran, Mr. Allen reads aloud from the teacher's manual as he gives the students their assignment: complete workbook pages 53 through 56. José, a student in the class, speaks little English and can only write in Spanish. Mr. Allen walks over and, using basic gestures, tells him to copy what his neighbor, Jack, writes down.

Later in the day, you run into Mr. Allen in the staff lounge and ask how José is doing. Mr. Allen casually replies, "I think he's doing fine. He doesn't say much."

"Is he able to do the work you assign?" you ask.

"I've just had him copy from his neighbor," Mr. Allen shrugs. "He doesn't seem to have any difficulty with that."

It's silent reading time in Miss Titus's class, yet the room is all *but* silent. Alex is out of his seat for the third time, getting a drink of water; Mae Lin and Maria are giggling and passing notes; and Tyler is locked in a tug-o'-war match with Chris over a book they both want to read. Miss Titus looks up from the papers she's grading at her desk, wearily tells Tyler and Chris to start reading, and then goes back to her work. This isn't how she envisioned her first year as a teacher would be.

Last night, she spent several hours prepping for today's reading lesson in which students would build papier-mâché boats to depict the ship in the story.

But what was supposed to be a fun and exciting activity turned out to be a fiasco. She spent the morning barking orders and reminding kids to follow directions. Now, she's exhausted, her room is in disarray, and survival mode has kicked in. Miss Titus is already counting down the days to the end of the school year.

At first glance, Mr. Allen's and Miss Titus's classrooms appear very different, but the trained coaching eye can identify important similarities. For one, both teachers have little awareness of best practices in teaching. In addition, neither has the ability to identify what is working and what isn't in their classroom, leading to a lack of accurate self-reflection. The focus in these classrooms is more on teaching tasks, such as assigning work and planning projects, than on individual student needs and whether learning is taking place. These teachers have the best of intentions, but they are missing the mark. Both Mr. Allen and Miss Titus embody the Unaware stage on the Continuum of Self-Reflection.

Common Descriptors of Unaware-Stage Teachers

Teachers in the Unaware stage misperceive the realities of their classrooms, students, and even instruction. When asked, they find it difficult to specifically identify what is working well and what isn't. When something isn't working, they are unable to address the issue because they are uncertain of the source of the problem and feel powerless to fix it. King and Kitchener (1994) identify these teachers as *absolutionists*, saying that they "tend to accept without question the culture they live in. They are in a comfortable position and are unaware that things could be different from how they are" (p. 48).

While many first-year teachers fall into this category, not all will. Furthermore, you may come across a 20-year veteran who falls in this category, as we did several years ago. Alisa recounts her story about that at the end of the chapter.

It is important to note that the Continuum simply provides an entry point for you as a coach. The characteristics listed in Figure 5.1 and discussed below should be used without prejudice to help determine your coaching strategy. There is no ideal key that will unlock every door (or teacher) you come across, but our goal is to offer a place to start, with the belief that if you take the steps to build relationships and individualize your coaching approach, the end result will be an increase in teacher capacity. In this way, using the Continuum of Self-Reflection is a critical strategy to effect meaningful, long-lasting school improvement.

Figure 5.1 Teachers in the Unaware Stage: The Continuum's Diagnostic Criteria	
Teacher's Reflective Tendencies	**Related Classroom Characteristics**
• Demonstrates little or no awareness of instructional reality in the classroom • Focuses on routine • Exhibits the best of intentions • Expresses confusion about own role in learning • Collaborates with colleagues on a superficial level • Defines problems inaccurately • Focuses on the job itself—the *act* of teaching	• Scripted lessons, with little or no teacher modeling • Passive learning, with little or no student interaction • Lessons built on direct instruction and assignments • Little or no evidence of systematic, standards-based planning • No differentiation of instruction • Little or no awareness of effective time management • No link between instruction and assessment • Little effort to make curriculum relevant to students

Reflective Tendencies

Teachers in the Unaware stage, like Mr. Allen and Miss Titus, may exhibit some (if not all) of the characteristics outlined here.

They demonstrate little or no awareness of instructional reality in the classroom. The term "withitness" has been used to describe "how well a teacher knows what is happening in all places at all times" (Loughran, 1996, p. 180). Unaware teachers are not aware that their instructional delivery is not working, that their students do not understand a concept, that their classroom management is ineffective, or that their curriculum focus is not linked to the required standards. They display little or no grasp of the instructional reality they experience every day, therefore lacking "withitness."

They focus on routine. Unaware teachers appear to be going through the motions, as if on cruise control in the slow lane. Their lesson delivery is outdated, and they show no signs of recognizing this fact or changing their teaching methods to accommodate the actual learners in their classrooms. Dewey reminds us that "routine action is guided by factors such as tradition, habit, and authority and by institutional definitions and expectations" (1933, p. 24). These teachers pass out the Pilgrims coloring packet every year before Thanksgiving because they have always done so. Every Friday, they follow the same script, giving a quiz, reading out the correct answers, and then asking students to call out their scores so that these can be recorded in the grade book. They do this because this is the routine their predecessor established, or a method they have used for many years.

They exhibit the best of intentions. These teachers desire to do a good job and really believe that they are doing so. There is no disingenuousness or insincerity in them. They are doing what they believe good teachers do. They are often the most misunderstood members on staff, easily judged on their limited perspective and antiquated ways.

They express confusion about their own role in learning. These teachers believe that authorities (i.e., the principal, a coach, the teacher's edition of the textbook) will tell them exactly what to do, and they do not really get what they, themselves, are supposed to bring. They expect "experts" to provide all the answers. They are confused when challenged to think and reflect about what takes place in their classrooms and to consider that they can possibly control the outcome.

They collaborate with colleagues on a superficial level. For teachers in the Unaware stage, the purpose of professional learning communities is unclear. In order to be able to collaborate with colleagues, teachers must know where they are going academically and the specific objectives they wish to accomplish with their students. There are so many things these teachers don't have a good handle on—from specific student needs to standards that must be met by the end of the year—that they're unable to participate fully in the PLC. When working in groups, they often contribute little to group growth and are much more likely to jump in to handle specific, task-oriented jobs, such as making copies, creating posters, or coordinating a grade-level field trip.

They define problems inaccurately. Miss Titus is frustrated and exhausted. Her classroom management is out of control and affecting student learning. Added to the chaos is the extra energy she spends each week planning creative lessons that lack purpose and structured focus. Ask her to define the problem, and she points a finger at her students. It is not that she is trying to shirk responsibility by passing the blame; rather, she does not have a complete understanding of the problem or of the role she might play in addressing it.

They focus on the job itself instead of the act of teaching. Ask Unaware teachers how they can tell if they are successful in their duties as teachers, and they are likely to point to the creative projects they have planned, the number of workbook pages they have completed, the bulletin boards they've decorated, the homework activities they have assigned, or even the number of snacks they give in a day. In their minds, good teaching is about completing these "teacher tasks"—checking off a set of prescribed activities.

Related Classroom Characteristics

Observing the following characteristics in a teacher's classroom may provide further indication that the teacher is in the Unaware stage of the Continuum of Self-Reflection.

Lessons are scripted, with little or no teacher modeling. Teacher's editions always in hand, Unaware teachers rely heavily on them to guide their day-to-day instruction. Any modeling that takes place usually comes right out of the scripted lesson in the teacher's guide. The teacher is more focused on finishing the daily lesson and accomplishing the tasks therein than in checking for understanding as the lesson proceeds.

Learning is passive, with little or no student interaction. Unaware teachers like Mr. Allen believe that the quiet student working independently is the kind of student who learns best, and their classroom management plans often reinforce this. They are not familiar with the research that supports active student engagement and the benefits of using cooperative learning strategies. Quite often, the direct instruction approach is the only instructional method these teachers know and use.

Lessons are built on direct instruction and assignments. With little or no awareness of effective instructional strategies to use while teaching, Unaware teachers spend most of their class time lecturing and assigning work for the students to complete. We call this the "I'm teaching, you must be learning" assumption. As Wong and Wong (1998) note in *The First Days of School*, in actuality, "learning has nothing to do with what the teacher covers; learning has to do with what the student accomplishes" (p. 210). Unaware teachers think only in terms of "covering" subject matter. Whether the students are learning or not is off their radar.

There is little or no evidence of systematic, standards-based planning. Unaware teachers' weekly plans are vague and linked only to the teacher's edition of the textbook. For some teachers, the plan book might even be blank. Lessons lack a specific goal or learning outcome, and often do not express a connection to grade-level or content-specific standards. Lessons are often random and do not appear to connect to one another or to a discernable unit or thematic plan. When asked to detail her plans for the week and share her rationale behind them (Why do you do what you do?), Miss Titus is unable to provide the particulars. Instead, she refers to her teacher's edition and goes off on a tangent about how excited she is for the elaborate project she has planned. Unaware teachers like Miss Titus can spend days planning and prepping for an assignment that has very few connections to the standards and in the end wind up with little to show for the time and energy they have invested.

There is no differentiation of instruction. Susie struggles with fluency; Matt stumbles when decoding longer vocabulary words. These observations mean little to teachers in the Unaware stage. Occasionally, they may come up with a shortened spelling list or fewer problems on the homework assignment, but there is no differentiated instructional approach. A teacher who recognizes that a student is struggling may assume it is because the student is not working hard enough and needs to be redirected to the task at hand. In order to differentiate instruction for their students, teachers need to be able to determine the students' individual ability levels. Because teachers in the Unaware stage don't pick up on variations in student readiness, they are unable to provide specific instruction that maximizes learning for all students in their classroom.

There is little or no awareness of effective time management. These teachers do not understand the idea that instructional time is a precious commodity. They will often spend lots of class time engaged in nonacademic activities, such as taking roll, doing a lunch count, and administering behavior reinforcement procedures. Their transitions do not take students quickly to the next learning opportunity. As Rutherford, Quinn, and Mathur (2007) put it, "An ineffective teacher may take 15 minutes to organize students and materials between two activities. Given that there are typically at least 15 transitions per day, these teachers lose a considerable amount of teaching time to managing student behavior" (p. 437).

There is no link between instruction and assessment. Unaware of the standards needing to be covered and the specific needs of their students, Unaware teachers may spend considerable time planning and implementing a lesson that had nothing to do with either. When they assess students, they do not make connections between specific students' learning needs and effective instruction.

There is little effort to make curriculum relevant to students. If you were to ask a couple of students in the Unaware teacher's classroom to describe what they are learning and why they are learning it, they would struggle to find an answer. Because the teacher makes little effort to provide a rationale for the activities assigned, students have no ownership over their own learning. They complete tasks and assignments because the teacher has asked them to.

The Coach's Goal

The overall goal for coaches of Unaware-stage teachers is to help them realize that change is needed and foster these teachers' desire to learn. Figure 5.2 provides an overview of a coach's role in building Unaware teachers' capacity for success and some recommended strategies for supporting their reflective growth.

The Coach's Role: Unconditional Partner

Like all learners, teachers in the Unaware stage need to feel respected and valued as individuals. Start by getting to know their strengths, limitations, and specific needs—recognizing their potential. This can only happen by developing an interpersonal relationship. Spend as much time as you can with teachers building trust and rapport. Share your own personal learning experiences as you work to create a collaborative environment as an unconditional partner.

As we've noted, teachers in the Unaware stage are often the most misjudged and underestimated individuals on staff, as it's easy to assume that they know better and are willfully ignoring best practices. Yet in most cases, these teachers simply don't know that they don't know. They're ignorant of better approaches, unskilled in effective strategies, and have limited knowledge of the resources available to them. They may also be some of the hardest workers on the staff, teachers who have received glowing reviews in the past, and teachers who are frequently requested by parents. However, on looking closely at the instruction and learning taking place in their classrooms, neither coach nor administrator can see much gain. Your role as a coach is to work alongside the Unaware teacher as an unconditional partner focused on helping that teacher build awareness of better practices.

Figure 5.2 Coaching the Unaware-Stage Teacher		
Capacity-Building Goal	**Your Role as Coach**	**Coaching Strategies That Foster Reflective Growth**
To create awareness of the need for change and foster a desire to learn	*Unconditional Partner* • Identify strengths, limitations, and needs • Recognize potential • Build trust through interpersonal relationships • Share your personal experience of becoming aware of different instructional strategies • Create a collaborative environment	• Visit the classroom • Seek additional opportunities to build rapport • Identify a specific instructional problem to build awareness around • Use specific questioning to establish rationales for teaching practices • Administer personal belief and reflective questionnaires • Provide opportunities to observe in other classrooms • Advocate journal keeping • Facilitate opportunities to exchange ideas with others during guided meetings

Strategies for Fostering Reflective Growth

There are a number of coaching strategies that will help you begin building a solid relationship with teaching staff in the Unaware stage.

Visit the classroom. As a coach, you will need to prove yourself to the Unaware teacher as one step in building trust and rapport. Start by offering to grade papers or hang a bulletin board, asking to use the classroom for an experiment, or offering to work one on one with a difficult student. This is an excellent way to show that you want to work alongside the teacher and aren't afraid to do the dirty work. In addition, this approach will create opportunities to model specific instructional strategies.

Seek additional opportunities to build rapport. You can create rapport by relating to people in a way that creates a climate of trust and understanding. Some ideas include joining the same committee, asking for help on one of your projects, inviting the teacher to coffee after work, sharing a book that you've just finished reading, or offering to copy papers or laminate materials. Rapport is integral to human communication and is critical to the cultivation and maintenance of positive relationships.

Identify a specific instructional problem to build awareness around. When you walk into the classroom of an Unaware teacher, you'll probably notice a multitude of instructional problems you'll want to address. Start by selecting just one. The goal is to build the teacher's awareness of this single instructional problem and then use it as the springboard for cultivating self-reflection and a more wide-ranging desire to learn. Once you have identified the target problem, stick with it; do not jump to something new until the teacher has addressed and resolved this problem to both your satisfaction.

Use specific questioning to establish rationales for teaching practices. Once you have established rapport with the teacher, you want to initiate thinking about his or her actions. You want to bring attention to the cause/effect relationships in his or her classroom. Start by asking a series of questions to lead to identification of the problem. Initially the responses you receive may be general and vague, but they will provide a base from which to offer further support and encourage the development of self-reflective thinking. Use the following questions as a guide:

- What worked well today? What didn't?
- What could have prompted Johnny to act up? Why do you think the students struggled with the homework? Why did Lara finish the book so quickly?
- What was your objective today during guided reading? What was your purpose for assigning the worksheet in math? Did your students learn what you wanted them to learn today? How do you know?
- What did you learn about Dennis from the assignment he just completed? What didn't you learn?
- What will you do differently tomorrow?

Administer personal belief and reflective questionnaires. Teachers' beliefs, values, and perspectives are products of personal life histories and are embedded into their professional practice. The more a teacher is aware of his or her personal beliefs, the more the teacher will reflect on his or her role in the classroom. Numerous belief and reflective questionnaires can be found online to help each teacher discover what he or she truly believes about the learning process.

Provide opportunities to observe in other classrooms. An Unaware teacher needs to see other teachers in action. After identifying a specific instructional strategy that you want to bring awareness to, strategically arrange for the teacher to observe in a classroom where another teacher is modeling this instructional approach. If possible, tag along and point out ways that the other teacher uses this particularly strategy to meet the specific needs of his or her students.

Advocate journal keeping. Writing our thoughts down is one of the most powerful forms of self-reflection. Ask the Unaware teacher to start by writing down feelings and thoughts at the end of each day. Pose some of the reflective questions listed on page 64, and if the teacher is interested, set aside some time to examine the contents of the journal together.

Facilitate opportunities to exchange ideas during guided meetings. Prior to a meeting, strategically ask each teacher to bring something specific to share. Arrange it so that the ideas address the specific issue that the Unaware teacher may be dealing with. The influx of ideas from colleagues might just spur the teacher to implement new practices and aspire to new reflective heights.

Alisa's Approach

When I first met "Sally," she was in her last year before retirement. I had been hired as an instructional coach and was new to the building. Sally was one of the first to warmly welcome me to the school, and I quickly noticed that she spent long hours working in her classroom. It wasn't long, though, before her name came up in casual conversation with a fellow teacher. The teacher was quick to point out that Sally was one of the most traditional teachers in the school and didn't know how to teach struggling students. "Be prepared; she isn't going to be open to anything you say," the teacher confided. "She's very stuck in her ways."

Over the first half of the year, I watched Sally make very little progress teaching reading to her group of students. Each time I popped by to see if she needed help, I was greeted with a big smile and a confident, "No, thanks!" By December, her class had made only half the amount of progress as the one next door.

I decided to try a new approach, and when we returned in January, I strategically traded spots with the classroom aide for an hour each day to get into Sally's classroom. For the next month or so, I worked unobtrusively alongside Sally, doing everything she asked. We started to develop a closer relationship, and I asked if she would mind me trying some new activities with the small group she had me working with. She agreeably gave me the go-ahead, and I noticed that she watched me closely that day.

The following morning, she stopped by my office. "I was amazed to hear the students in your group read that higher-level book yesterday," Sally told me. "And I couldn't believe the deep discussion you had with them. I never knew my kids could have such in-depth conversation, and I'd like to try doing what you did. Will you show me what to do?"

Sally and I worked closely for the remainder of the year. She started a reflective journal documenting the progress of her reading group. As she grew in her awareness of best-practice strategies, she became eager to learn more. I arranged for her to observe other colleagues in action and asked her to share her new learning with the rest of the grade-level team. What I had considered "resistance" early on was simply a long-standing unawareness of better practices.

The Unaware Stage at a Glance

Teachers in the Unaware stage are not "bad" teachers; they merely lack awareness of best practices and have a limited repertoire of skills. As a result, they tend to gravitate toward more traditional approaches to teaching and more traditional views of learning. They see no reason to change the way they do things simply because they are unaware of the need to do so. By cultivating a strong relationship and gently bringing problem areas to their attention through the use of the strategies listed, you can build instructional awareness and work to meet our goal of making the most of each individual teacher's capacity and potential.

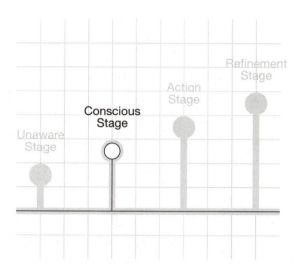

6

The Conscious Stage

Think for a moment of a personal habit that you would like to change. Perhaps you want to quit smoking, eat better, exercise more, or save more money. You know it will improve your life to do so. Now imagine yourself making this life change. Does it happen overnight? If you're like the majority of us, it doesn't. That's why we don't have a planet full of perfect people. At one time or another, we all can identify something that we should and could change about ourselves but don't. Regardless of the reason for our lack of follow-through, we are still "good" people with the potential to change should the right catalyst come along. Keep this analogy in mind as we examine teachers in the Conscious stage of the Continuum of Self-Reflection.

Meet the Teachers

Here's a look inside the classrooms of some Conscious-stage teachers.

Every year, Mrs. Williams teaches a language arts unit on her favorite book, *Where the Red Fern Grows*. The class reads the book aloud using the round-robin reading method. The book is too difficult for several students; she skips over them when it's their turn. Mrs. Williams periodically stops the class and calls on individual students to answer a couple of comprehension questions before they resume with the oral reading.

Mrs. Williams attended several trainings last year on literature circles and participated in a teacher book club on *Improving Instruction with Think-Aloud Strategies* (Wilhelm, 2001). She was excited at the beginning of the year to implement some of what she had learned, but the first quarter is almost over and there is no evidence yet of this best-practice instruction. When you ask her about using differentiated instruction with literature circles, Mrs. Williams explains that it is too difficult to implement in her classroom: "I tried the grouping thing, but it didn't work for me. I have too many different levels in my class. I know it's not the best, but I'm going to stick with what I know. It's just too much work to start small groups with the group of kids that I have. I might give it a try in the spring."

It's the last week of the second academic quarter, and you pop into Mr. Bissonnette's room to help him analyze his quarterly reading assessment scores. As you begin to talk about the data, you discover that Mr. Bissonnette speculated on the reading levels of his students when he placed them in their current reading groups. Several have scored significantly higher than the level of book they are currently reading, and five students have been reading books that are much too difficult for them.

When you bring the discrepancy to his attention, Mr. Bissonnette sheepishly admits that he is aware of the problem. He has been meaning to make the needed changes in his reading groups but hasn't gotten around to it yet. He plans to have new reading groups in place by Monday. A week later, you stop by and find that his students are still working in the same misassigned reading groups. Mr. Bissonnette is quick to provide you with the excuse that he arrived to work a little late this morning and left his list of new reading groups at home. He figured one more day in the old reading groups wouldn't hurt. He assures you he'll have the new reading groups in place by the end of the week.

As Mrs. Williams and Mr. Bissonnette talk about instruction and what *should* be taking place in their classrooms, it may seem that they are on their way to becoming self-reflective individuals. They are aware of best-practice instruction and can talk about what they hope to accomplish in their classrooms. They attempt to set instructional goals and often ask for suggestions. These behaviors are promising. Yet, over time, something doesn't quite add up. Mrs. Williams and Mr. Bissonnette are in the Conscious stage on the Continuum of Self-Reflection.

Common Descriptors of Conscious-Stage Teachers

Teachers in the Conscious stage are aware of best-practice instruction and what they should be doing in their classroom. They have read about, attended workshops on, and perhaps even observed colleagues using these research-based methods. Yet, for whatever the reason, there is a disconnect between what they know and talk about and the reality taking place each day in the classroom. When asked to describe their daily instruction, Conscious teachers can easily provide a detailed account of what occurs, but what they describe and what's actually taking place are two different things. These teachers know what they should be doing, but they lack the motivation, ownership, buy-in, follow-through, discipline, accountability, or clear vision to consistently apply what they know.

The instructional decisions made in Conscious teachers' classrooms each day are ultimately made to fulfill their needs rather than the needs of their students. Like teachers in the Unaware stage, Conscious teachers can be quick to assign blame when things don't go as planned. The difference is that Conscious teachers are aware that the problem lies with their instructional approach and use blame as a way to excuse poor performance. The Continuum of Self-Reflection provides diagnostic criteria that can help you identify teachers in this stage (see Figure 6.1) and begin to motivate them to bring their knowledge and actions together.

Reflective Tendencies

Teachers in the Conscious stage, like Mrs. Williams and Mr. Bissonnette, may exhibit some (if not all) of the tendencies that follow.

They demonstrate a consistent "knowing–doing" gap. Conscious-stage teachers may not be expert in best-practice instructional strategies, but they are aware of the difference between what works and what doesn't. A teacher may know, for example, that research has shown round-robin reading to be one of the least productive strategies for teaching reading yet may continue to implement the technique. A teacher may know that he or she should preview the chapter ahead of time and write down meaningful comprehension questions to guide the discussion and yet neglect to take the time to do so, choosing to make up questions along the way instead.

Figure 6.1
Teachers in the Conscious Stage: **The Continuum's Diagnostic Criteria**

Teacher's Reflective Tendencies	**Related Classroom Characteristics**
• Demonstrates a consistent "knowing–doing" gap • Can ambiguously cite research to support current teaching methods • Makes excuses for problems • Demonstrates limited ability to evaluate problems • Becomes easily distracted from goals • Collaborates inconsistently with colleagues • Disregards others' ideas • Focuses first on *self*	• Instruction designed for teacher convenience • Short-term planning evident yet inconsistent • Occasional links between instruction and assessment • Little student engagement in active, meaningful learning • Little problem solving from students • Occasional differentiation of instruction • Noticeable swings in instructional approaches

They ambiguously cite research to support their current teaching methods. Conscious teachers want to connect their current way of teaching to evidence-supported strategies. They may do this by making vague references to research or by selectively seeking out and citing research that backs up what they are doing in their classroom. In other words, rather than approach research with an open mind, looking to learn from it, Conscious teachers single out only that which validates their way of doing things in an attempt to justify their actions. This approach is reminiscent of a quote attributed to legendary Los Angeles Dodgers broadcaster Vin Scully, who shuddered at those who "use data the way a drunk uses a lamppost: for support, not illumination."

They make excuses for problems. "I'm not grouping my students for reading because I have too many levels and not enough books," Mrs. Williams justified earlier in this chapter. Instead of taking personal responsibility for the instructional decisions made in the classroom, Conscious teachers often place blame in an attempt to justify their actions. Blame will fall on students, parents, a lack of resources, or a lack of support.

They demonstrate limited ability to evaluate problems. Rosa is struggling to keep up with the rest of the class in reading. A Conscious teacher might make the hasty assumption that Rosa's struggle is attributable to her limited English skills and move to address this problem by assigning additional worksheets from the English language learner workbook. In reality, Rosa has difficulty with fluency, and with specific strategy-driven instruction, her reading competency would improve dramatically. It requires a healthy does of patience and diligence to analyze a problem and find the best solution. Conscious teachers tend to diagnose problems quickly (and often inaccurately), decide on a solution (often the easiest one), and proceed from there.

They become easily distracted from goals. The awareness that they should be doing something differently in their classroom drives these teachers to occasionally set goals to make changes. However, as Mrs. Williams showed, these goals are easily brushed aside when the rubber meets the road. The difficulty for a coach working with teachers in the Conscious stage may not be getting them to set a goal, but getting them to pursue a focused path, follow through, and ultimately accomplish the goal they have set.

They collaborate inconsistently with colleagues. Whether Conscious-stage teachers show it or not, they recognize that they are not doing all that they can when it comes to delivering instruction in the classroom. A natural consequence is that they withdraw from the relationships that they feel will hold them accountable for their practices. Conscious teachers can be the most social members of the school staff, but they will keep relationships lighthearted and focus conversation on the baseball scores or the quality of the grub in the cafeteria. These teachers can avoid topics that might require deep thought, vulnerability, and professional collaboration.

They disregard others' ideas. Conscious teachers are caught in the knowing–doing gap, and as a result, they take a defensive stance toward others who may come forward with suggestions or ideas. To these teachers, any idea incongruent with their own beliefs and approaches is treated like an invasion — worthy of fighting off, dismissing, and ignoring.

Their first focus is themselves. For Conscious teachers, it's "all about me," rather than about effective instruction, professional responsibilities, or (most important) student learning. These teachers do what works for them. A Conscious teacher who doesn't feel like calling reading groups on a particular day may pass out a packet of worksheets or do an art project instead. Conscious teachers' regard for the needs of their students takes a backseat to their own job satisfaction.

Related Classroom Characteristics

Observing the following characteristics in a teacher's classroom may provide further indication that the teacher is in the Conscious stage of the Continuum of Self-Reflection.

Instruction is designed for teacher convenience. Although Mr. Bissonnette knew that his students were reading books that were too easy or too difficult for them, he did nothing about it. It was more convenient for him to keep the students in the same groups, or to hand out the same book to the entire class, than it was to arrive at work a few minutes earlier and make the necessary changes. In conversation with the instructional coach, Mr. Bissonnette reveals that he has the best of intentions, yet he needs accountability to follow through consistently and do what he knows is right. In his book *Readings for Reflective Teaching*, Andrew Pollard says, "They may be satisfied with having established a particular formula for teaching which keeps the children quiet and occupied, but then fail to look critically at what learning is taking place" (2002, p. 38).

Short-term planning is evident yet inconsistent. These teachers know they need to plan but struggle with mustering up the energy and focus it takes to create a long-term unit or yearly block plan. Instead, they will implement short-term plans that are often very thoughtful and meaningful. Observing the classroom of a Conscious teacher, a coach will occasionally see a week that is built upon solid lesson planning followed by a week without much direction.

There are occasional links between assessment and instruction. It is not an easy task to link assessment and instruction, and teachers in the Conscious stage struggle to bring the two together, often because they haven't invested the time necessary to do so. Looking at a class list chock full of assessment data can be overwhelming, and while they know in theory that their instruction should be based on what they learn from the assessments, they also don't intuitively understand what to do to make it fit. An excellent way to help these teachers make the connections needed and build a solid instructional focus is to collaborate with them as they write their weekly lesson plans. Feiman-Nemser and Buchmann (1987) point out that there often is a vast gulf that exists between "going through the motions of teaching . . . and connecting these activities to what pupils should be learning over time" (p. 257).

There is little student involvement in active, meaningful learning. When you walk into the classroom of a teacher in the Conscious stage, you are likely to see students either sitting passively at their desks listening to the teacher or working on "time-filler" activities, with the teacher disengaged. Active, meaningful learning requires active, meaningful planning. Conscious-stage teachers do not always have the focus and motivation to consistently put together engaging, rigorous lessons. Coaches must be willing to spend a good deal of time on a daily or weekly basis helping them develop plans in order to make significant progress.

Students aren't asked to take the lead in problem solving. The fact is, telling others what to do requires less energy and is much easier than showing them. For teachers in the Conscious stage, this is an uncomplicated and appealing way to get through the day. Unfortunately, solving problems for students is an easy habit for many to get into, regardless of the stage they're in, and it is a habit that takes intentionality to break. Coaches must build awareness of this habit, offer better strategies, and provide consistent feedback to bring about effective change.

Instruction is occasionally differentiated. Patty is an emergent reader, Monica is functioning at grade level, and Raúl can't be challenged enough. It takes thoughtful and systematic planning to meet the specific needs of such diverse students, and these teachers struggle to be effective in this area. Differentiated instruction is a best-practice approach that must be used if students are going to learn. Conscious teachers know that they need to differentiate, and they may occasionally make an attempt to do so—for example, assigning a tiered activity now and then or pulling a student aside for a special lesson—but there is no systematic approach or long-term planning behind this individualized instruction.

There are noticeable "swings" in instructional approaches. A teacher in the Conscious stage may be excited to implement literature circles one minute, then talking about the importance of skill-based instruction and walking students through the English textbook the next. Conscious teachers are drawn toward new and exciting ideas, only to find that the work behind solid implementation is too much. They then jump ship and try the next "fun" idea they see. This is a small-scale manifestation of the unfortunate practice of "educational faddism."

The Coach's Goal

The overall capacity-building goal for Conscious-stage teachers is to motivate them and show them how to apply pedagogical knowledge consistently. Figure 6.2 provides an overview of a coach's role related to Conscious teachers and some recommended strategies for supporting their reflective growth.

Figure 6.2 Coaching the Conscious-Stage Teacher		
Capacity-Building Goal	**Your Role as Coach**	**Coaching Strategies That Foster Reflective Growth***
To motivate and show how to apply pedagogical knowledge consistently	*Motivator and Strategist* • Praise generously • Reach out to include teacher in collaborative work • Communicate and maintain a clear vision • Build confidence through short-term goal setting • Focus on small changes • Make daily contact, checking in often to talk about goals and progress toward them	• Provide daily feedback highlighting instructional strengths • Examine and discuss student data • Develop a detailed action plan • Focus on short-term, attainable goals that will have long-term impact • Provide support for instructional goals and best-practice strategies • Meet weekly for collaborative lesson planning (guided planning) • Model specific techniques and provide ample time for discussion • Design meetings around a specific instructional topic

*Employ Unaware-stage coaching strategies as needed.

The Coach's Role: Motivator and Strategist

Regardless of the stage a teacher is in, the coach should always begin by building a solid relationship founded in trust. You can have the best of intentions and use a variety of approaches, but if the teacher does not trust you, you will be unsuccessful in everything you try to accomplish. Teachers in the Conscious stage are likely to be the most challenging in this respect. You will need to spend more time and put forth more effort and energy to develop and sustain relationships with these teachers than with teachers in any other stage of the Continuum. If you have not spent an adequate amount of time fostering your relationship with a Conscious-stage teacher before jumping in and offering suggestions, you run the risk not only of failing but of making the teacher more reluctant about and defiant toward change.

So, build relationships with Conscious teachers carefully. As we note, they are aware of their need to change but are very sensitive when others notice and bring it to their attention. Start by making daily contact with teachers and going out of your way to be inclusive. You might pop in and compliment a new haircut or praise a new instructional approach you recently observed. Check in often to build a friendship and encourage efforts toward positive change. The Conscious teacher needs to know that he or she matters to someone else. We caution you to be sincere in your interactions. It is easy to spot a disingenuous person, and this too can damage any relationship. Be generous with your praise as you talk about goals and the progress made toward them. As you strategize together, focus on small, specific changes that the teacher can easily make and communicate a clear vision—what you're working toward and how you plan to get there. In these ways, you can maximize teacher performance and tap into each individual's unique potential.

Strategies for Fostering Reflective Growth

There are a number of coaching strategies that will help you gently motivate and encourage teachers in the Conscious stage to set specific, achievable goals and experience the power that comes when they follow through.

Provide daily feedback highlighting instructional strengths. This can be as simple as complimenting the teacher on using an active engagement strategy when you pop into the room during the day to drop something off. Before we jump in and try to "fix" what is broken, we need to recognize what works; in doing so, we build rapport and trust. The teacher will be much more likely to listen when we suggest an alternate way of doing things if we have first recognized what they do well.

Examine and discuss student data. In his book *Results*, Mike Schmoker attests, "Data make the invisible visible, revealing strengths and weaknesses that are easily concealed" (1999, p. 44). The Conscious teacher is less likely to become defensive when the focus is on student performance rather than teacher performance. This can be achieved by looking at general classroom assessment data and pinpointing a subject area to focus on.

Develop a detailed action plan. When this teacher is working toward a goal, has a clear idea of what is expected of him or her, and knows exactly how to get there, the chances of success multiply tremendously. For many, a simple action plan is all that is needed. Action plans come in all shapes and sizes but should contain these essential components: quarterly goal, evidence that the goal will have an impact on student achievement, the standards addressed, current student data, best practice-based activities or strategies leading to goal achievement, the coach's support role, and evidence of goal success. "[Developing] clear goals and [determining] ways to assess progress toward them are highly effective in reducing 'teacher uncertainty'" (Rosenholtz, 1991, p. 13).

Focus on short-term, attainable goals that will have long-term impact. This teacher needs to taste the intrinsic feeling that comes with setting a goal, working toward it, and achieving it. Start small and simple, and do everything within your power to foster success. The teacher will succeed in fulfilling his or her initial long-term goal with the help of the short-term targets you set together along the way. Hoover (1994) noted that when student teachers were given a predetermined focus, they demonstrated more reflectivity. When given student teaching assignments without a focus, they tended to respond with complaints about their teaching experience, their mentor teachers, and the reality of the school setting.

Provide support for instructional goals and best-practice strategies. This approach works well for the teacher who exhibits initial reluctance to the call for change. More often than not, a teacher in the Conscious stage needs more information, like specific research and assessment data, to be able to process the need for change and begin to take action. Providing support also means stressing the importance of knowing why we do what we do. This teacher needs to be drawn back to this fundamental question throughout the day, week, and year. After all, "coaches who participate in a search for answers are modeling the idea that finding answers to the needs posed by the students in a classroom is what good teachers do" (Storms, Riazantseva, & Gentile, 2000, pp. 26–27).

Meet weekly for collaborative lesson planning (guided planning). This strategy is an excellent place to start when working with a teacher in the Conscious stage. Not only does it allow you to meet with the teacher on a weekly basis, it will allow you to quickly get a feel for the instruction taking place in the classroom. Conversations over lesson plans lend themselves to reflection and can easily be guided toward a specific instructional goal.

Model specific techniques and provide ample time for discussion. Teachers in the Conscious stage need to see what they are working toward before they can make it their own. That said, do not expect this teacher to watch a technique just once before trying it out. A teacher in this stage needs repeated modeling. Providing ample one-on-one time to discuss the process individually is also essential. This teacher needs to ask questions, be encouraged to challenge the answers, and discover how to make the new technique his or her own.

Design meetings around a specific instructional topic. Organize a grade-level or subject-area meeting around a specific topic. For instance, ask teachers to bring questions, ideas, and examples of teaching the element of voice in writing. Beforehand, ask a few teachers to read a specific research-based article and share it with the group. Your goal is to build knowledge and validity around a specific topic while at the same time building collegiality among a group of teachers.

Alisa's Approach

"Oliver" was new to the district, hired at our school to teach 5th grade. He'd arrived with a smart-looking résumé that showed experience in all of the intermediate grades, and his most recent position was as a school administrator. He was a social, likable person, and he quickly hit it off with the staff. In my first conversation with Oliver he impressed me with his knowledge of teaching reading and his plans to differentiate instruction.

A month into the year, however, I realized that Oliver's classroom looked very different from what I had expected. There was no differentiation of instruction going on, and students would spend more than half of the reading block working on spelling from an old, outdated workbook. When I asked Oliver about his long-term plans in reading, his reaction was immediate and defensive. He explained to me that he didn't feel his kids were ready to move into small groups yet, "and anyway, I once read a research article on the link between spelling and reading. Looking at their reading scores, I think my kids need this practice."

I smiled and quickly changed the subject, knowing that we did not have a strong enough relationship to continue the conversation further. I now needed to make an effort to pop into Oliver's classroom each day to build rapport and highlight the positive things I observed.

It wasn't until the end of the following quarter that I felt we had reached the point where I could bring up the topic of change without receiving a defensive reaction. I used the quarterly reading data from Oliver's class to guide our conversation and made sure to keep the focus on student progress rather than on Oliver's classroom instruction itself. Then I casually asked if he had ever heard of reciprocal teaching, explaining that I had recently read a great deal of research that supported the strategy and was looking for a classroom in which to try it out.

He agreed to allow me to teach his reading block each day for 45 minutes and consented to continue to use the strategy after I got things going. The first four weeks went well. I set up reciprocal teaching groups and taught the students how to work in them, and we were off to a fantastic start.

Then it came time for Oliver to begin to take over and continue what I had started. I was very optimistic . . . but that feeling didn't last long. He grew increasingly frustrated with the new "system" and was struggling to keep it together. We met on several occasions and discussed the rationale behind using this instructional strategy, going over specific questions he had. Yet each day, Oliver became increasingly resistant, negative, and distant.

I was at a loss as to what to do, until I realized that he was resistant because he was fearful of failing what I had started. He didn't have the confidence yet to move forward and tackle this new approach. I had thrown it at him before he was fully ready.

The following day, I met with Oliver and asked if I could continue working in his room for several more months while he gradually assumed responsibility of the rest of the elements. Without hesitation, he agreed, and my new work centered on developing his confidence in tackling what he knew to be a best practice. Over time, this Conscious-stage teacher became one of the leading proponents of reciprocal teaching in our school. His students have reaped the benefits, and he has thanked me repeatedly for helping him overcome the "knowing–doing" gap that he was caught in.

The Conscious Stage at a Glance

Everyone has had the experience of owning a favorite pair of jeans or a t-shirt that has acquired sentimental value over time. Time and wear may have taken their toll, but regardless of the holes and frayed edges, this piece of clothing remains special. It is an "old friend" whose presence makes us feel more comfortable in the world around us. Good sense tells us to replace the old with the new, but something inside rebels against the notion. We fear the new won't be as good as the old; it won't provide us with the same comfort that we're used to.

Whether we like to admit it or not, we all have holed up for a moment (or a decade or two) in the Conscious stage. It doesn't make us bad; it makes us human. More than teachers in any other stage, teachers in the Conscious stage of the Continuum need a coach's daily encouragement and support. They need us to recognize their potential and gently guide them down the path of self-reflection.

7

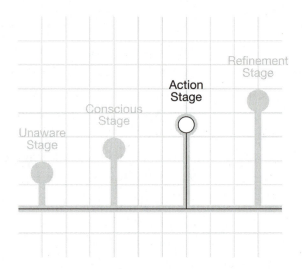

The Action Stage

The most successful people in any profession have one thing in common: *They get things done.* Pick up any self-help book, read any inspirational article, or watch any interview with a prominent person, and you'll find that all of them will tell you that taking action is the only way to accomplish anything in life. A quick look back at the 2007 Amazon best-seller list attests to the desire we have to take action and make changes to improve our lives. Included in the top 100 titles are *Getting Things Done: The Art of Stress-Free Productivity, Your Best Life Now!, The 7 Habits of Highly Effective People, Become a Better You,* and *Women and Money: Owning the Power to Control Your Destiny.* Nevertheless, the reality is that even though we seem to know that improvement is something to strive for, taking the steps to achieve it is difficult (thus the existence of self-help books, personal trainers, and financial advisors!). The moment we realize this truth and elect to make the necessary changes that will help us move toward our goals, we step into the Action stage on the Continuum of Self-Reflection.

Meet the Teachers

Let's visit with some Active-stage teachers.

"Where do I start?"

It's Monday morning, and Ms. Taylor corners you in the staff lounge with this seemingly random cry for help. Further explanation sheds some light: She is struggling to provide appropriate instruction to her American History class. The students whiz through the textbook and any supplemental materials she places in front of them but cannot answer simple comprehension questions about what they've read. You arrange to come in and observe the class the following day and then model several reading comprehension lessons for Ms. Taylor later in the week.

The lessons go well, and Ms. Taylor is enthusiastic about implementing the new ideas you have shared. But two weeks later, she appears again. "I've been teaching what you showed me, and my students are using the strategies!" she exclaims. "I just don't know where to go next. Can you come in again?"

Mr. Bartlett, who has been teaching for two years, approaches you one day to share his concern about several students who are struggling with reading. Since the inception of his leveled guided-reading groups, all but three of his students have made significant progress. He's frustrated because guided reading is a best-practice strategy, and he doesn't know what he is doing wrong and why he isn't reaching those last three kids.

After a lengthy discussion and several days' observation in his classroom, you suggest that these particular students may benefit more from a structured, phonics-based approach. Mr. Bartlett hesitates: "I know readers need phonics, but I have always been under the assumption that phonics-based programs were wrong. Kids learn to decode but can't comprehend. What would a phonics-based approach look like? How would my guided-reading groups change?"

Ms. Taylor and Mr. Bartlett have taken two critical steps in their journey of self-reflective growth. First, they recognized a problem and made the decision to do something about it. Second, they realized that the work they faced was a bit beyond their current capabilities, so they sought assistance and ideas from their instructional coach. Their actions are much like those of an individual who looks in the mirror one day and decides that it's time to live a healthier life but still needs the strategies, reminders, and motivation of a fitness consultant to make that goal a reality. A key difference between teachers in the Action stage and their colleagues in the Conscious stage is that Action teachers are more likely to practice what they preach, to walk their talk. And when they realize their limitations, they ask for further help.

Common Descriptors of Action-Stage Teachers

"Where do I start?" and "Where do I go from here?" are the most common questions of teachers in the Action stage. They have developed a genuine awareness of problems associated with student learning in their classrooms, have taken responsibility for those issues, and are motivated and ready to respond to them. They just don't clearly see how to go about it.

These teachers are usually approachable, receptive, and open to outside influence as they embark on their quest for the "right way to do things." Often unable to see beyond the lesson they are teaching, Action-stage teachers don't know where to go next. They will frequently address problems by latching onto the first solution that makes sense. They need expert guidance and direction as they become skilled in new methods and learn to discern the difference between instructional strategies that are grounded in research and those that are not. Regardless of the years they've put into the profession, they may not have the confidence that experience brings. However, they do have the commitment to make lasting, positive changes.

The Continuum of Self-Reflection provides diagnostic criteria that can help you identify teachers in this stage (see Figure 7.1) and begin to design your coaching strategy.

Reflective Tendencies

Teachers in the Action stage, like Ms. Taylor and Mr. Bartlett, will exhibit some (if not all) of these tendencies.

They accept responsibility for the success of all students and for their own personal growth. Psychologist Carl Rogers once said, "The curious paradox is that when I accept myself just as I am, then I can change" (Blaydes, 2003, p. 87). He was right on the mark. Being able to accept responsibility for what happens in the classroom requires a considerable amount of personal awareness and self-acceptance as teachers openly recognize that they can change and improve as professionals. In his book *The 7 Habits of Highly Effective People*, Stephen Covey

(1989) asserts that all things are created twice: We create them first in our minds, and then we work to bring them into physical existence. Accepting responsibility is the first shift Action teachers take toward active self-reflection.

Figure 7.1
Teachers in the Action Stage: **The Continuum's Diagnostic Criteria**

Teacher's Reflective Tendencies	Related Classroom Characteristics
• Accepts responsibility for the success of all students and for own personal growth • Evaluates issues and situations objectively • Seeks to incorporate research-based concepts and strategies • Reflects upon teaching only after the action • Believes in only one "right" way of doing things • Struggles to identify solutions to long-term problems • Receives feedback well, then enters a critical loop • Collaborates on a limited basis with colleagues • Focuses on the *science* of teaching	• Regular use of assessment to monitor student progress • Consistent application of best-practice instructional strategies • Lessons linked to standards • Evidence of limited long-term planning • Classroom appears functional, but gaps are lurking

They evaluate issues and situations objectively. Action teachers see a problem and make an attempt to "fix" it. This is the defining moment for them—they have embraced the idea that they can improve and are now ready to act upon their belief. After gathering information and analyzing the situation, these teachers may not always be able to pinpoint the exact solution, but they are determined to make changes toward improvement.

They seek to incorporate research-based concepts and strategies. When they realize that something is "wrong," Action teachers want to respond with the "right" solution. They recognize that there is a higher standard of teaching, based on research, that they can attain. They desire to better themselves and seek to learn more about best-practice research through attending professional workshops, reading books and articles, or seeking the guidance of an instructional coach.

They reflect on their teaching only after taking action. Action teachers do not have the schema in place to be able to reflect and respond before or during a lesson. After trying something new, they will look back, reflect, and make

83

necessary changes the next time they attempt that particular instructional strategy. The act of reflection itself is delayed, making them more reactive teachers than proactive ones.

They believe in only one "right" way of doing things. Once Action-stage teachers discover a new strategy that works, it can be difficult to convince them that alternate approaches can be equally effective. In their pursuit to develop mastery of a best-practice instructional approach, they become committed to a single point of view, tending to see the world in black/white or good/bad terms. William Perry, author of "Cognitive and Ethical Growth," defines this reflective characteristic as "cognitive egocentrism" (1981, p. 87). These teachers find it difficult to entertain points of view other than the ones they embrace themselves.

They struggle to identify solutions to long-term problems. Action teachers are easily frustrated with students who do not respond to the new best-practice strategy they are trying. They have difficulty recognizing why it isn't working. Their limited knowledge and experience lead to a narrow understanding of larger problems (i.e., they cannot grasp the "big picture"), and they lack the ability to discern what the right solution may be.

They receive feedback well, then enter a critical loop. Mistakes are an essential part of learning and developing. These teachers see fault in their own instructional approach and quite rightly want to improve upon it. However, once they start to improve themselves, it becomes easy for them to feel that others should be making the same changes. A coach should gently remind Action teachers that change is a process and encourage them to be patient with themselves and their colleagues. They will be more likely to influence others if they, themselves, are accepting of the differences they see.

They collaborate with colleagues on a limited basis. It takes a great deal of motivation and energy to change and grow as a professional. Typical Action teachers are rather egocentric as they work to improve themselves. And while they may desire to collaborate more with colleagues, they have little energy left to do so. Additionally, because they have difficulty embracing others' points of view, the collaboration is generally superficial and can leave many collective issues unresolved.

They focus on the science of teaching. The primary focus for Action teachers is on the science of teaching. Many of their thoughts, discussions, reading, and ideas revolve around the concepts of instructional pedagogy and classroom decision making. They are interested in learning and implementing best practices in their classroom and are quite aware of the effect of evidence-based teaching on their students' learning.

Related Classroom Characteristics

Observing the following characteristics in a teacher's classroom may provide further indication that the teacher is in the Action stage of the Continuum of Self-Reflection.

Assessment is regularly used to monitor student progress. Action-stage teachers want to know if their instructional approach is working and if their students are learning. They rely on frequent assessments, mostly formal tools, to monitor academic growth. After each assessment interval, they evaluate their instructional progress and attempt to make necessary changes in order to increase student achievement.

Best-practice instructional strategies are consistently applied. It is readily apparent that these teachers are making a sincere effort to do what is best for their students. Whether you notice a transformation in the classroom environment (more student-generated work, desk clusters for cooperative learning, etc.) or changes in specific instructional approaches (differentiated instruction, the use of active engagement strategies, etc.), once Action teachers have resolved to make changes toward improvement, you will see minimal relapse into old habits and ways.

Lessons are linked to standards. These teachers may not have "I can" statements posted each day in their room, objectives written on the board, or standards systematically recorded in their lesson plans, but they are aware of what needs to be taught and have an objective for each lesson. Classroom activities and assignments also point clearly to the stated learning targets. Action teachers make a concerted effort to link instruction with the standards they are responsible for teaching.

There is evidence of limited long-term planning. Action teachers have written long-term and daily plans for student learning that follow a logical and developmental sequence. The plans, however, are generally limited to individual subject areas and do not connect one context or subject area with another, which reduces their overall effectiveness. With such a narrow focus, Action teachers limit their own ability to succeed.

The classroom appears functional, but gaps are lurking. Walk into the classroom of an Action teacher any day of the week and you will see evidence of attempted best-practice strategies. These teachers are working hard to increase and expand their repertoire of skills, and it shows. But upon closer observation, you might see lessons that could be built upon but haven't been, teachable moments that are overlooked, and a random order to the introduction of best-practice lessons. These subtle discrepancies reflect a limited instructional perspective, primarily attributable to a lack of experience or comprehensive knowledge.

The Coach's Goal

The overall goal for Action-stage teachers is to help them to build on their experience and strengthen their expertise. Figure 7.2 provides an overview of a coach's role related to Action teachers and some recommended strategies for supporting their reflective growth.

The Coach's Role: Mentor

When you want to learn something new, pick up a new hobby, or become skilled in a new trade, what kind of trainer do you seek out? Without a doubt, it's an expert in the field who is knowledgeable enough to teach what you need to know. You want someone who has a lot of experience and can pass along a few tricks of the trade. You want a person who can acknowledge not having all the answers but does have the resources and skills to help you find the answers you seek.

But expertise alone does not make a good coach. You also want someone who knows how to educate others, someone with the ability to know when and how to release responsibility and let you take charge of your learning. At some point in time, the ski instructor must step back and allow novice skiers to try a run on their own; a pianist must allow the student to play unaccompanied.

Action teachers are looking for that knowledgeable, expert mentor. They are eager for new ideas and will readily try what you (the mentor) suggest. But at the

	Figure 7.2	
	Coaching the Action-Stage Teacher	
Capacity-Building Goal	**Your Role as Coach**	**Coaching Strategies That Foster Reflective Growth**
To build on experience and help strengthen expertise	*Mentor* • Validate ideas, actions, and instructional decisions • Release responsibility and encourage independence • Provide research from which to construct meaning • Model open-mindedness toward multiple approaches and perspectives • Collaboratively engage in diagnosis and action planning	• Invite participation in small-group discussions • Use the Apprenticeship Model • Use classroom observation and provide specific feedback • Videotape and analyze performance together • Foster idea sharing through collegial observations • Use reflective questioning • Create a dialogue journal • Encourage participation in a professional book club • Encourage workshop attendance as a way to share learning • Analyze individual student data together • Publicly recognize expertise • Help develop a system for storing and organizing information

same time, it is essential that you (as the mentor) gradually release responsibility for the learning and focus the majority of your coaching on building necessary critical thinking and discernment skills.

You can begin by validating the teachers' ideas, actions, and instructional decisions. These teachers want to know they are doing things right. Beware of them becoming too dependent on your expertise, though. Engage them in the process of diagnosing problems, researching solutions, and creating action plans to develop competence and discernment, which are essential reflective characteristics. Action teachers will readily latch onto the first solution that they find, so it is important to provide ample research that supports multiple approaches to the same problem. Once a successful strategy has been found, it can be easy to disregard all other strategies. A coach must model holding and defending a point of view while exhibiting tolerance for other points of view. A reflective teacher is one who is open-minded and always ready to learn something new.

Strategies for Fostering Reflective Growth

Action-stage teachers will be the most inquisitive and receptive teachers you work with. Here are some specific coaching strategies to help you gradually shift into a mentoring role.

Invite participation in small-group discussions. Considerable research has been published on the effectiveness of professional learning communities, and the teachers who will benefit the most from participating in these learning teams are the ones in the Action stage. There are various ways to organize these groups, from random, informal gatherings to highly structured PLC teams. As a coach, identify a common concern or topic of interest shared by a group of teachers and arrange a discussion. Ask teachers to bring student data and plan to provide a myriad of informative resources that will help guide the investigative process, such as professional books, related articles, applicable videos, and anything else that might be beneficial.

Use the Apprenticeship Model. In their book *Issues in Mentoring,* Trevor Kerry and Ann Shelton Mayes (1995) describe the Apprenticeship Model as a coach working alongside a teacher, following a coteaching structure: "In order to be able to 'see,' trainees need an interpreter. They need to work alongside a mentor who can explain the significance of what is happening in the classroom" (p. 18). The power in this approach is that the coach can provide insight the exact moment that it may be needed, instead of bringing it to light after the fact.

Conduct classroom observations and provide specific feedback. Ask any room full of instructional coaches to describe what they do, and most of them will include the practice of observing teachers and providing feedback on their instruction. You'll notice this strategy has been absent from the chapters addressing previous stages of the Continuum, however; we saved it for Action teachers. Unless a teacher in another stage specifically requests observation and feedback, we strongly encourage you to confine your use of classroom observation to teachers in this stage. Why? Because a coach in the position to observe and provide feedback comes close to acting as an evaluator. It is essential that you steer as far away from that role as possible, and you can do so by adhering to the following advice:

• Prior to observing, sit down with the teacher and determine together what you will provide feedback on.

• When writing your feedback, include ample examples of positive things that you see taking place.

• Always conference with the teacher and provide feedback in person. Do not leave written feedback for teachers to interpret by themselves.

Videotape and analyze performance together. Most teachers never get the opportunity to watch themselves in action. Doing so provides an unusual perspective that can lead to deep reflection. Instructional coaches are in the unique position of being able to provide this as an option to facilitate the analysis of specific instructional strategies and real-time decision making. Bailey, Curtis, and Nunan (1998) studied the use of videotaping as a means to promote reflective teaching and improvement and came to this conclusion: "We maintain that [videotaping] with trusted colleagues in a collaborative approach to reflective teaching can definitely promote professional development" (p. 546).

Foster idea sharing through collegial observations. There is ample research to support peer observation as a successful form of professional development as well as a powerful component in the reflection process, yet teachers rarely have the opportunity to visit other classrooms. Again, the instructional coach is uniquely able to provide this option. Set up a time to cover a teacher's class so the teacher can visit another. If at all possible, strategically pick both the classroom and the specific lesson the teacher will observe, matching both with the observing teacher's individual goal. (And always make sure you pre-arrange this with the other teacher involved.) This is not to be an evaluative observation; rather, the other teacher should be touted as an expert in the focus area.

Use reflective questioning. Action-stage teachers are often unsure which questions to ask after a lesson, or they might have a list of questions ready but not know what to do with the answers. It is our first tendency as "experts" to provide solutions to the issues these teachers share with us. Yet, as experts, we must be aware of teachers' need to think for themselves. Asking open-ended, reflective questions instead of providing ready answers will cultivate critical thinking and nurture independence.

Create a dialogue journal (coach and teacher or team journal). Yinger and Clark (1981) believe that writing reflective notes is more powerful than reporting them orally. Try setting up a dialogue journal between yourself and the teacher in which you both record and respond to questions and reflections directly and immediately. You might also set up a team journal centered on a specific topic and encourage all team members to contribute and respond to each other's reflective thinking. To strengthen the collective learning, the team can meet on a regular basis to debrief their thoughts and engage in deeper discussions.

Encourage participation in a professional book club. Action teachers want to become experts, and participating in a professional book club or study group is an excellent way to become one. Bandura's theory of social learning holds that "environments that promote interpersonal interaction result in greater reflection" (1977, p. 22). Set up any group (a grade-level team, a subject-area department, or even a purely random assortment of teachers) with a book that is relevant to current issues they are dealing with and organize a consistent time to meet each week. The key is to keep the topic of the book applicable to existing instructional issues and to ask a different member of the group to lead the discussion at every meeting. Take yourself out of the driver's seat—sit back, participate, and enjoy watching these teachers shine!

Encourage workshop attendance as a way to share learning. Today's educational climate is laden with workshops and conferences featuring the biggest and brightest names in the field sharing their expertise. It won't be difficult to find one near your zip code that relates to your Action teachers' instructional focuses. Training sessions that yield the greatest benefit are those that the teacher and coach attend together, as reflection is more effective when two people share the same experience and can debrief one another. As a coach, you can then create opportunities for teachers to share what they learned with the staff upon return—again, removing yourself from the limelight and subtly empowering the teachers to be the experts.

Analyze individual student data together. One of your goals as a coach is to cultivate a deeper understanding and appreciation of multiple best-practice approaches. You can do so by inviting Action teachers to identify several students in their classes who are making the least amount of growth—students for whom the current best-practice instructional strategy isn't working. Together, analyze student data and create individual action plans using alternate instructional approaches. Journaling comes in handy here. Ask teachers to track student responses to the new approach and record personal reflections along the way.

Publicly recognize expertise as often as possible. Good coaches work behind the scenes to make everyone around them look good. After working closely with Action teachers on specific instructional strategies, arrange for other teachers to go in and observe what they are doing. Invite your Action teachers to share what they have learned at a department meeting. Organize a schoolwide professional development day and ask them to lead sessions on specific topics of expertise. Create a bulletin board in the staff lounge where they can highlight instructional strategies they are currently putting into practice.

Help develop a system for storing and organizing information. As Action teachers take steps to learn more and improve their professional practice, they will begin to collect a mass of research articles, books, lesson plan ideas, and reflective notes. Encourage them to set up a filing system to organize information as they gather it. The information they collect will become an invaluable resource over the years, and it is vital that they establish a maintenance system for these important items.

Alisa's Approach

It was the beginning of the school year, and "Meloney," a third-year teacher in the Action stage, asked if we could meet. Over the previous two years, she and I had spent quite a bit of time together working to establish solid classroom management techniques, and she was finally gaining the upper hand. So I was surprised when Meloney burst out with this: "I really want to be a good teacher, Alisa, and I've done quite a bit of thinking over the summer. I need you to be brutally honest with me and tell me everything I need to do to improve. You're always so nice and encouraging. I need you to come into my room this year and tell me exactly what I'm doing wrong. Don't worry about hurting my feelings."

"What makes you think that you're doing things wrong?" I asked.

"I don't feel like I really have a handle on what I'm doing each day. I don't know where I'm going with my lessons. I don't know what to teach next. It's hard to think that I'm doing anything right," she admitted openly.

It was then that I realized that the problem wasn't that Meloney needed to know what she was doing wrong; it was that she needed to build confidence in what she was doing right.

I used a variety of reflective questions to engage her in an exploration of the instructional areas that she felt "good" about. When we got to the subject of lesson planning, she readily admitted that she struggled with them. So we set up a plan to start the year by meeting once a week to put together her lesson plans; at the same time, we created a dialogue journal that we could use to pose reflective questions and record thoughts linking our planning to the actual events and learning of each day. At the end of the first quarter, Meloney and I met and looked at the assessment data from her class. The data reflected significant gains, which she attributed to her newfound skill of creating systematic, focused lesson plans. By December, Meloney's confidence in her teaching had increased tenfold.

The Action Stage at a Glance

A teacher in the Action stage can be compared to a novice rock climber who has just learned the basics of the sport and is ready to climb that first mountain. Can the climber make it to the top without the help of an instructor? Most likely, yes. But will he or she climb more efficiently and become skilled more quickly with an instructor offering guidance along the way? Absolutely! Can Action teachers, likewise, build their repertoire of skills and develop experience without the help of an instructional coach? By all means, yes. But they will learn to teach more effectively and strengthen their expertise more efficiently with an instructional coach guiding them along the way. Our job as coaches is clear. We must steer teachers in the Action stage to become experts on their own as they build an appreciation of extensive instructional strategies and develop important critical thinking skills.

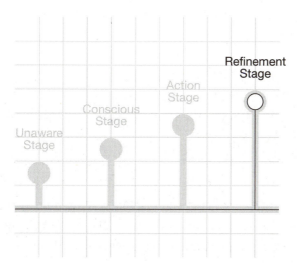

Unaware
Stage

Conscious
Stage

Action
Stage

Refinement
Stage

8

The Refinement Stage

One of the first rules new drivers learn is "Follow the speed limit." But is adhering to that rule always the right or wise thing to do? How about when the speed limit on the freeway is 65 miles per hour, but traffic is moving at 75 miles per hour? Or when road conditions are icy and the visibility is minimal? And what about one of the most basic rules parents give their children: "Don't talk to strangers." Does this rule apply the first time the children meet Great-Aunt Margaret, or the new babysitter, or the new soccer coach? Does it apply when they're lost in the shopping mall? Clearly, there are times when doing the "right" thing is wrong and doing the "wrong" thing is right.

Consider the following classroom. The teacher, a highly motivated, knowledgeable individual, has extensive training in best-practice strategies, which are the foundation for the classroom's operation. Every activity is backed up with research validating its use and promising higher achievement. There's no doubt the students are learning, and at significant rates. But is it possible that not *all* students are making the same considerable gains? Could a child ever walk in the doors of this classroom and *not* succeed? The answer is yes.

As teachers develop the ability to critically reflect on their own practice, they will come to understand that there are times when the "right" way to do something will not work. Which way is "right" is conditionally affected by the variables of the situation. Teachers who arrive at this state of understanding and have the ability to shift their thinking and actions in response to such variables have entered the Refinement stage on the Continuum of Self-Reflection.

Meet the Teachers

Here's a look inside the classrooms of some Refinement-stage teachers.

Mrs. Nelson introduces the learning outcome of today's lesson on fractions by folding paper. The students watch as she folds a large piece of paper in half, discusses the fraction, and then folds the paper again. After several minutes of modeling and discussion, Mrs. Nelson asks the students to take their own papers and fold them to show a specific fraction. Immediately she sees that Henry and a few others are having difficulty, and she realizes that they are not ready to move to guided practice. Deviating from her plans, she asks the students to partner up and practice making specific folds with additional sheets of paper. Then she calls Henry and the other struggling students over to a table, where she provides additional modeling using fraction blocks as well as heavy support with the paper-folding exercise. Ten minutes later, the small group is on track and ready to rejoin the rest of the class. The math lesson continues without skipping a beat.

Two years ago, Mr. Sutter's school district adopted a new language arts program. His principal announced that every teacher should implement the series in its entirety. While some teachers took this directive to mean that they must adhere to the daily script found in the teacher's manual and use every worksheet provided, Mr. Sutter understood that the publisher did not intend for the program to be used in this manner. He maintains fidelity to the program without running a scripted, worksheet-driven classroom. For example, rather than passing out the vocabulary worksheet, he might divide his class into groups and have them play a vocabulary game using the words from the lesson. Instead of calling on students one at a time to answer the story questions in the teacher's guide, he might ask them to choose a partner and sketch their responses. The teacher's guide provides the scope and sequence, and Mr. Sutter works to implement various instructional strategies to help all his students achieve the learning outcomes.

Mrs. Nelson and Mr. Sutter are focused on doing what is best for each student in their classroom rather than what is best for the sake of pure teaching, the adopted program, or even themselves. Their embrace of the saying, "If the children aren't learning, we aren't teaching," places them in the Refinement stage on the Continuum of Self-Reflection.

Common Descriptors of Refinement-Stage Teachers

Refinement teachers have reached cognitive maturity. They have an extensive amount of knowledge and experience that form a large frame of reference around their profession. Yet for these teachers, teaching is not about knowing and becoming skilled at the research-based "rules" that good teachers follow; rather, it is about revealing the "exceptions"—understanding the individual child they are working with and discovering what he or she needs to learn. These teachers are adept at research-based instructional strategies, but they also understand that those best-practice strategies are subject to a multitude of variables and may occasionally need to be swapped out for other, less supported approaches. Their inquiry-based practice, to quote Henderson's Reflective Teaching Model, "emphasizes an ethic of caring, a constructivist approach to teaching, and creative problem solving" (1992, p. 7).

Refinement teachers stand in front of a classroom of 25 children and see 25 unique individuals bringing 25 different experiences and perspectives to the table. They see 25 distinct personality and learning styles, each defined by diverse strengths and weaknesses. There is no perfect research study that can tell Refinement teachers exactly what strategies will meet the unique needs of every child who walks in the door, but they don't look for one that will. For every strategy used, there is the possibility that the student will respond in a different way. They know that in a classroom full of children, the variables are endless.

In their book *No Quick Fix*, Richard Allington and Sean Walmsley (1995) state, "There is an enormous range of differences in children when they begin school. This suggests that the quantity, quality, and intensity of instruction needed for children to become literate with their peers will differ. We need to think of individual differences less as indicators of how much or how little children might learn, and instead think of them as an indication of how much intensive instruction will be needed to accelerate their literacy development and move them alongside their peers" (p. 6). Jeffrey E. Porter (2006) agrees: "No blueprints, no formulas exist for determining which instructional approach will support which learner in mastering which learning outcome in which discipline area" (p. 55). We'll borrow some of Brookfield's words to describe Refinement teachers as they endeavor to support the learning of each student: they act as "interpretive, not ballroom" dancers (1995, p. 139).

The Continuum of Self-Reflection provides diagnostic criteria that can help you identify teachers in this stage (see Figure 8.1) and begin to craft a suitable, individualized coaching approach for them.

Figure 8.1
Teachers in the Refinement Stage: **The Continuum's Diagnostic Criteria**

Teacher's Reflective Tendencies	Related Classroom Characteristics
• Reflects before, during, and after taking action • Recognizes that there are multiple "right" courses of action • Maintains a vast repertoire of instructional strategies • Engages in action research as common practice • Modifies lessons and plans to meet students' needs • Pursues opportunities to work and learn with colleagues • Thinks beyond the classroom • Focuses on the *art* of teaching	• Assessment drives daily instruction • Students largely responsible for their own learning • Multiple instructional strategies in use

Reflective Tendencies

Teachers in the Refinement stage, like Mrs. Nelson and Mr. Sutter, may exhibit some (if not all) of the tendencies that follow.

They reflect before, during, and after taking action. Refinement teachers interpret, analyze, and find solutions to problems before, after, and—most significantly—*during* lessons. They can also reflect within multiple time frames at any given moment. For example, toward the end of a math lesson, a Refinement teacher may realize that several students do not understand the learning outcome and decide to alter the instructional approach immediately to accommodate the students' needs. While doing so, the teacher may remember that last year's class was further along in the book by this time in the year but, on reflection, decide against changing the pace of instruction. In this way, they illustrate Pollard's description of reflective teaching as "a cyclical or spiraling process, in which teachers monitor, evaluate, and revise their own practice continuously" (2002, p. 17).

They recognize that there are multiple "right" courses of action. Refinement teachers are characterized by their open-mindedness. Dewey defined this characteristic as "an active desire to listen to more sides than one, to give heed to facts from whatever source they come, to give full attention to alternative possibilities, to recognize the possibility of error even in the beliefs which are dearest to us" (1933, p. 29). These teachers know that the knowledge base they currently draw from may change with the introduction of new information. They view learning as an ongoing, unfolding, evolving activity and understand that their beliefs and knowledge will grow throughout their lifetime.

They maintain a vast repertoire of instructional strategies. As Pollard puts it, "Reflective teaching requires competence in methods of evidence-based classroom inquiry, to support the progressive development of higher standards of teaching" (2002, p. 17). Refinement teachers have a considerable amount of varied instructional strategies in their toolbox to pull out at a moment's notice. Without a doubt, they are considered extraordinary instructors.

They engage in action research as common practice. Schön (1983) notes, "When someone reflects-in-action, he becomes a researcher in the practical context. He is not dependent on the categories of established theory and technique, but constructs a new theory of the unique case" (p. 68). Refinement-stage teachers first identify a problem: "Beth is not meeting the reading growth goals." Next, they analyze current assessment data and make a hypothesis: "Her fluency scores are low. I'm going to work with her group on phrasing and expression strategies." Finally, they look to see if the strategy is working; if it's not, they revise their approach: "Beth's fluency scores have increased slightly but not dramatically. I'm going to pull her for an additional 10 minutes a day to work one on one."

They modify lessons and plans to meet students' needs. Refinement teachers are always thinking outside the box when it comes to student learning. When assessment results indicate that there are gaps in knowledge, these teachers will adapt already-written lesson plans to address those gaps. For instance, if students in a biology class miss many of the vocabulary-based questions on an assessment, their teacher may decide to create a motivational vocabulary game and add it to the agenda.

They pursue opportunities to work and learn with colleagues. Relationships are an essential part of the process of reflection for Refinement teachers. Eager to capitalize on the knowledge and expertise of their colleagues, they seek out opportunities to share ideas, discuss pedagogy, unearth thoughts, and debate philosophy. To quote the insightful words of Stephen Brookfield (1995), they see collaborative inquiry with professional peers as "a challenging, passionate, and creative activity" (p. 1).

They think globally, beyond the classroom. These teachers involve themselves in tasks and projects that benefit more than just the students in their classroom. They may volunteer to be on the School Improvement Planning Committee, the supply committee, or a team that develops the school Web site. They are willing to take initiative, have long-term vision and want to make their school a better place. As John Gabriel (2005) describes, this kind of teacher "doesn't deal in scraps; she deals in what is best for all students and teachers" (p. 19).

They focus on the art of teaching. For Refinement teachers, teaching is not about knowing and following all of the rules of evidence-based instruction; it is about understanding the child that they are working with and providing the instruction necessary for that child to learn. These teachers are thrilled by discovering the nuances of teaching. They desire simply to facilitate and maximize the learning of everyone within their sphere of influence: themselves, their students, and their peers. Barnes (1992) claims that, "when asked what it is that [they] teach, they] won't reply, 'English, sociology, or auto mechanics,' [they'll] say, 'people'" (p. 14).

Classroom Characteristics

Observing the following characteristics in a teacher's classroom may provide further indication that the teacher is in the Refinement stage of the Continuum of Self-Reflection.

Assessment drives daily instruction. Assessment that does not lead to intelligent instructional decisions is pointless at best and destructive at worst. While

Action teachers use occasional benchmark-type assessments to determine if their instructional approach is working, Refinement teachers use daily, informal assessments of each student to chart and adjust the instructional direction of each lesson.

Students are responsible for their own learning. In the classrooms of Refinement teachers, you will see students setting personal goals and tracking their progress and the teacher monitoring this ongoing progress and using the insight it provides to guide instruction. They know, as Angelo and Cross (1993) put it, that "the most effective assessment strategies for figuring out how best to support student learning are those developed and implemented by teachers and students themselves in answering their own learning/teaching questions, not those prescribed by someone's packaged wisdom about types of learners and teacher-proof instructional strategies" (p. 73).

Multiple instructional strategies are in use. In *What Works in Schools: Translating Research into Action*, Robert J. Marzano (2003) states, "It is perhaps self-evident that more effective teachers use more effective instructional strategies. It is probably also true that effective teachers have more instructional strategies at their disposal" (p. 78). Refinement-stage teachers are aware of the individual abilities of their students and deliberately use various instructional strategies and creative assignments to tap into each child's potential, being careful to actively engage and support all students at all times. And self-evident as it may be, it's still worth mentioning that this sort of "instructional effectiveness" is yet another identifier of a highly effective teacher (McEwan, 2001).

The Coach's Goal

The overall goal for Refinement-stage teachers is to encourage these teachers' long-term growth and continued reflection. Figure 8.2 provides an overview of a coach's role related to Refinement teachers and some recommended strategies for supporting their reflective growth.

The Coach's Role: Collaborator

Teachers in the Refinement stage are highly motivated, highly reflective individuals. For them, there is promise in every class period, potential in every

	Figure 8.2	
	Coaching the Refinement-Stage Teacher	
Capacity-Building Goal	**Your Role as Coach**	**Coaching Strategies That Foster Reflective Growth**
To encourage long-term growth and continued reflection	*Collaborator* • Compliment creativity and originality • Bring attention to hard work • Stimulate discussions of personal vision and educational philosophy • Practice "mirror-listening" • Ask questions to drive personal reflection and growth	• Provide a wide range of pedagogical resources • Encourage book club facilitation or initiation • Analyze group data together • Establish a team action research project • Encourage conference participation and publication submission • Arrange for student-teacher hosting opportunities • Promote talent development • Encourage leadership

student, and new learning around every bend. Challenges and opportunities for growth empower these teachers along their path. In a poetic sense, the journey is their destination.

As a coach, it is easy to think that Refinement teachers do not need help or support; after all, they are already engaged in the process of self-reflection. Yet the idea that these teachers have arrived at their ultimate destination or the notion that "once in a state of reflection, always in a state of reflection" couldn't be further from the truth. The foundational belief in the theory of reflection is that there is always room for improvement. These teachers need a coach as much as anyone else does; however, the coach works with teachers in this stage as a collaborator. John Murray, professor of higher education administration at Texas Tech, says, "While transformative learning begins in self-reflection, it requires a community to sustain it" (2005, para. 6).

Start your coaching work with Refinement teachers by complimenting the creativity and originality that you see in their classroom. These teachers put a lot of time and energy into what they do, and their achievement is worthy of attention. Stimulate them further by talking about personal visions and educational philosophies, which are the things that drive us to do what we do each day.

The more Refinement teachers engage in the process of reflective teaching, the more they increases their competence. In order to encourage long-term growth and continued reflection, ask open-ended questions and practice "mirror-listening": highlighting what teachers share rather than trying to interpret their remarks or leading with your own thoughts. In this way, as a coach-turned-collaborator, you can participate in the reflective process alongside teachers, embarking on a joint venture of learning and reflecting together.

Strategies for Fostering Reflective Growth

Here are some coaching strategies to help you initiate collaborative opportunities with teachers in the Refinement stage and encourage them to continue in their state of reflection.

Provide a wide range of pedagogical resources. Teachers in the Refinement stage need to continue to expand their minds and challenge their beliefs. A coach might pass along a journal article on interventions for transitional readers as a "fun read" or locate a book discussing Shakespeare's use of typical human traits for a teacher that requested such a resource. A journal article, online video, Web page, or professional book can broaden teachers' perspective on a topic and provide examples beyond those that a coach can articulate. This also provides a common ground on which coaches and teachers can base further conversation and reflective growth.

Encourage professional book club facilitation or initiation. In order to successfully facilitate a book club, one must be thoroughly familiar with the content presented, as well as skilled in the art of discussion. This can present new challenges to teachers who are new to the role of peer leader. The alternate approach is to initiate a group-led book club. Teachers can approach their colleagues or post an invitation in the staff lounge to participate in a group-led discussion. One person can be the organizer, but the group shares responsibility for leading the conversation each week.

Analyze group data together. This strategy works best when you pull together a small team of teachers in the Refinement stage. With schoolwide assessment data in hand, encourage the group to use systematic, inductive thinking to identify specific patterns and relationships in the data and to go on to extricate some generalizations. For example, after looking at their second-quarter schoolwide reading data, one group of teachers realized that girls had a greater increase in reading growth than boys did, especially in grades 4–6. After bringing these data to the attention of the leadership team, it was determined that more high-interest/low-readability books were needed in the classrooms. Involving Refinement teachers in activities like this not only develops their critical thinking skills but also encourages continued reflection on a global level.

Establish a team action research project. The goal of action research is to identify an area of concern and develop and conduct a new approach in order to address it. When Refinement teachers get together and tackle an issue, the synergy created has great potential not only to motivate the participants but also to enhance the culture of the school. This strategy can be used with other teachers on the Continuum as well, although we recommend including at least one Refinement teacher in the consortium.

Encourage participation in conferences, seminars, and publications. Refinement teachers have expertise and reflective experiences to share. Identify specific areas of strength and encourage teachers to submit a proposal to present at a conference or write an article for an educational publication. (Ask teachers to co-present with colleagues if they are hesitant.) Organize a mini educational conference within your building and ask Refinement teachers to lead a presentation or discussion with the staff at your site. By doing so, you can encourage and challenge these teachers to become educational leaders and influence student achievement outside their classroom.

Arrange for student-teacher hosting opportunities. What better way to reflect upon your own practices than by having an aspiring teacher in your room? Not only must Refinement teachers model exemplary instructional practices and strategies, but they have a responsibility to mentor and coach student teachers, observing lessons and offering feedback and constructive criticism (Gabriel, 2005). This relationship forces both mentor and student to engage in ongoing self-reflection.

Seek out opportunities for individual talent development. Capitalizing on Refinement teachers' strengths is essential for the growth of the school community, as they can make significant differences in the culture and climate of their school (Gabriel, 2005). A Refinement teacher who is passionate about teaching writing should not be pushed to become an expert in math strategies. Instead, a collaborative coach should encourage the teacher to pursue mastery of subject areas and instructional strategies that he or she enjoys and feels competent in, and then create opportunities for teachers to share their expertise with others.

Encourage leadership (if this is a strength). Leadership in education is a fickle beast, and not every talented teacher has aspirations beyond the classroom. Many Refinement teachers have no desire to present in front of a room full of people, yet most would be more than willing to host a student teacher or mentor a rookie colleague. If working in the spotlight is not appealing, there are plenty of behind-the-scenes opportunities to exert influence that can be encouraged instead.

Alisa's Approach

I was intimidated by "Herman" from the start. He was efficient and effective and had more experience than I. So it was with much trepidation that I entered his classroom for the first time to offer my "services" as a new instructional coach. Herman was very accommodating and listened intently as I recited all the ways that I could support him as a teacher. At the end of my speech, he casually said, "Sure, you can come in and model a lesson if you want."

The following week, there I was, modeling a writing lesson for Herman, who had little if any personal connection to what I was doing. At the end of the lesson, he thanked me and said something to the effect of, "It's always good to see someone else teach." I walked away feeling *somewhat* satisfied that I had done my job by passing along new insight to this not-at-all-needy teacher. Yet the rest of that school year, Herman continued to be an enigma to me. I never knew exactly what he wanted from me and always felt that what I was providing wasn't helpful.

It wasn't until I began work on the Continuum of Self-Reflection that I realized that Herman was in the Refinement stage. He didn't need me in his classroom as a coach or an expert; what he needed was someone to listen to and collaborate with him. Armed with that new knowledge, I marched into his room the following year and began with a couple of heartfelt compliments on his knowledge of best practices and thanks for his patience with me the previous year.

As we talked, Herman warmed up and began to share what he enjoyed the most in teaching: working with struggling readers. It occurred to me that he was a valuable resource who needed to be sharing his expertise with others. I asked if he would open his classroom up to other teachers for observation during his reading block. He agreed. The following quarter, I encouraged him to organize a grade-level book club using a book that he and I had referred to on several occasions. In the spring, Herman hosted his first student teacher.

Herman wasn't the only person to grow professionally that year. His student teacher, grade-level colleagues, and (more poignantly) I were *all* challenged to reflect upon our practices.

The Refinement Stage at a Glance

Most people are unaware that Russian novelist Leo Tolstoy had a keen interest in education. Over the course of his life, he built more than 70 schools and went on to say this about educators in the classroom: "The best teacher will be he who has, at his tongue's end, the explanation of what it is that is bothering the pupil. These explanations give the teacher the knowledge of the greatest possible number of methods, the ability of inventing new methods and, above all, not a blind adherence to one method but the conviction that all methods are one-sided, and that the best method would be the one which would answer best to all the possible difficulties incurred by a pupil. That is, not a method, but an art and a talent" (quoted in Schön, 1987, p. 66). Mr. Tolstoy, in all his wisdom, has given us yet another eloquent definition of a teacher in the Refinement stage.

Part III

The Enduring Work of Building Administrators

To excel as an administrator you must never forget that each of your direct reports is unique and that your chief responsibility is not to eradicate this uniqueness, but rather to arrange roles, responsibilities, and expectations so that you can capitalize upon it. The more you perfect this skill, the more effectively you will turn talents into performance.

—Marcus Buckingham

In their pursuit of excellence and continuous improvement, school administrators face challenges, obstacles, pressures, constraints, and unexpected impediments. Fortunately, the results, when they come, are well worth the struggle required to achieve them. Another light at the end of the tunnel is the understanding that the building administrator is arguably the most influential variable in education today. The administrator has the ability to inspire, encourage, and activate the potential and output of every single teacher on staff. It is true that accomplishing this task requires a vast repertoire of skills and expertise. First and foremost, he or she must tackle cultivating relationships and building teachers' capacity for success.

Here in Part III, we offer a framework for the administrator's role in Strength-Based School Improvement, beginning with roles and responsibilities (Chapter 9) and continuing with the essential behaviors required to supervise teachers (Chapter 10), a model of an observational walk-through (Chapter 11), and the art of providing meaningful feedback to teachers (Chapter 12). We wrap up with Chapter 13's look at the critical links among differentiated supervision, teacher evaluations, and ongoing, embedded professional development options.

Although Part III could stand alone as a resource to guide school administrators' work with individual teachers, it works best as part of our larger implementation involving both administrators and coaches. Coordinating the administrator's efforts and approaches with those of the coach yields more durable relationships, more consistent professional growth among staff, and more dependable advancements in student achievement.

9

Introduction to the Administrator's Role

In Chapter 2, we discussed how establishing meaningful relationships in schools requires strong leadership. We also introduced the definitions of *leadership* and *management* as they relate to school improvement. Marcus Buckingham (2005), a noted expert on leadership and management, shares this advice: "You can play both roles, of course, but if you do, you must know when to change gears. When you want to manage, begin with the person. When you want to lead, begin with the picture of where you are headed" (p. 71).

The school administrator happens to be assigned just that exact, wonderfully unique, special responsibility. In many cases, the administrator is in charge of at least 50-some employees, shouldering the load of acting as leader *and* manager of the whole organization. In Strength-Based School Improvement, the administrator must provide what Buckingham considers the leader's "universal vision," as well as determine the correct approach to motivating and managing each individual employee . . . and must do both well.

What's an Administrator to Do?

The position of school administrator is arguably the most demanding and most influential role in American education today. Here in the Era of Accountability, the challenges and pressures that building administrators face—including heightened public scrutiny, sanctions for underperformance, and budgetary constraints—accompany some drastic changes in the educational landscape and force today's administrators to make some difficult choices (Hall, 2006b).

Faced with innumerable choices about how to spend their time, and with so much riding on every decision and every course of action, administrators have to allocate every minute wisely. As 30-plus-year veteran educator Kim Marshall (2006) asks, "What's a principal to do?" How *should* principals (or any school administrators) spend their time?

To answer that question appropriately, let's follow the backward-design model and first identify goals for administrators. The administrator shares two overarching goals with the instructional coach: *to build teacher capacity* and *to increase student achievement*. It would follow logically that administrators should engage in behaviors that will lead directly to the accomplishment of those goals.

What are those behaviors? Which actions most closely correlate with building teacher capacity and increasing student achievement? This is where the rubber meets the road. Teachers and other instructional staff are a school administrator's most valuable and useful assets. As we've observed, they are a school's true strength. The classrooms are where they do what they do. Ergo, administrators should spend the lion's share of their time in the classrooms with the teachers and instructional staff.

Prioritization

As simple as that last sentence sounds, in practice it is an immensely difficult concept to carry out. The daily demands of parent meetings, student discipline incidents, bus stop patrols, incessant phone calls, paperwork, and e-mails and the disasters that hit the front office on a daily basis are substantial obstacles that can bog down even the most deft administrator. So how can we prioritize our time and our decision making to maximize the minutes we spend engaged in the behaviors that matter most? Let's consult with Stephen Covey (1989), author of *The 7 Habits of Highly Effective People*, and consider his Time Management Matrix (see Figure 9.1).

Every action and event that occurs in an administrator's day fits into one of the quadrants found in the matrix. A trusted colleague once told us that when we consider this matrix, we can call the items in Quadrant I "fires," and the only "fire" that's *really* a fire is an actual fire! Although there are other circumstances that fit the description of high-urgency, high-importance events—medical emergencies and dangerous intruders on campus fit the bill, for instance—if we keep "fire" in mind, we'll remember that these are the events that *force* us to stop whatever we're doing and attend to them, no matter what, because life and death could hinge on our reactions.

Quadrant II activities are very important, which means they relate to the results that link daily work with the school's mission and vision. However, they are not terribly urgent. These are tasks that we need to accomplish, but they don't need to be done *right now*. Activities such as cultivating the school vision, building relationships among staff members, and engaging in professional development work match these criteria.

Quadrant III tasks need to be accomplished now, but they don't really relate directly to the accomplishment of the mission and vision of the school, nor do they support the goals of the school administrator. Most of the tasks that we find ourselves engrossed in match this definition: answering phone calls, reading and responding to e-mails, completing paperwork, creating schedules, conducting discipline investigations, and so on. Do these tasks sound familiar? If so, that's because a tremendous amount of our energy goes into conducting this sort of routine, typical business.

Figure 9.1
Covey's Time Management Matrix

	Urgent	Not Urgent
Important	**Quadrant I**	**Quadrant II**
Not Important	**Quadrant III**	**Quadrant IV**

Quadrant IV activities are of low urgency and low importance. They don't really require our energy or attention, and in fact we have come to refer to these items as "handoffs." These are tasks that should be delegated. Someone other than the administrator could handle them without a problem. Ordering books for the school library, writing the letter inviting students to summer school, coordinating fundraisers, decorating bulletin boards, and brewing coffee for the staff room might fit into this category.

Clearly, the secret to lasting school improvement won't be found in Quadrant IV. Neither is it in Quadrant I (fires) or Quadrant III (not related to the mission and vision of the school). It is Quadrant II work that is key to school improvement. This is where the action is, and this is where administrators should spend their time. But with all the non-Quadrant II stuff that piles on the administrator's desk, how can effective administrators redirect their attention and focus on Quadrant II?

Quadrant II: If Not Now, When?

Remember that Quadrant II tasks—cultivating the school vision, building relationships among staff members, and engaging in professional development work—are extremely important to the growth and development of the school for a variety of reasons, but they are not necessarily urgent—things we *need* to engage in *right now*.

But if not now, when? Consider for a moment the other categories of the matrix. We react to the Quadrant I fires because we have to. We react to the Quadrant III phone calls, e-mails, and reports because we're used to reacting to them; this is what school administration has always been about. We even get suckered into reacting to the Quadrant IV tasks that we should hand off, because administrators are notoriously reluctant to give up control and are often firm believers in the old maxim that "if you want it done right, do it yourself." But because there's nothing to react to with regard to Quadrant II tasks, the ultra-important work often goes undone. If we really want to realize school improvement, truly wish to maximize our teachers' potential, and honestly desire to increase student achievement, we must proactively engage in Quadrant II behaviors. These are the activities that will yield results. This is where we achieve our mission and vision.

Saying no to all the other tasks and prioritizing Quadrant II work is not an easy thing to do. It requires us to step out of our comfort zones and rethink the status quo. It demands that we exact an incredible amount of self-discipline. Depending on our own ability to budget time and handle all the jobs required of us, it may mean setting aside time during the day to intentionally walk this talk. We have to be willing to say, "Strength-Based School Improvement is the most important, most beneficial activity I can be doing right now. So here I go."

The Administrator's Responsibilities

Having read Part II of this book, you know about the Continuum of Self-Reflection, a tool for getting to know teachers and designing an appropriate coaching plan for them. If you have an instructional coach on your staff, collaborate, share notes, and reflect together in order to get a baseline Continuum designation for each teacher. Discuss the common goals you'll be working on. (And refer frequently to the administrator's model of the Continuum of Self-Reflection, which we'll get to in Chapter 12.) We cannot stress enough how important teamwork is in this respect: Your job is to work *together* to bring out all your teachers have to offer.

What are the administrator's specific responsibilities and practices that will help accomplish the lofty goals of Strength-Based School Improvement? What are the specific Quadrant II activities that will lead to increased teacher capacity and increased student achievement? We have identified and outlined these key behaviors and have gathered them together in a model we call the Administrator's Responsibilities Diamond (see Figure 9.2). In the next four chapters, we will explore each of the Diamond's four facets in detail, providing examples and offering a model that any school administrator can put into place immediately—and start to see immediate results.

Facet 1: Individual Relationships

In Chapter 10, we discuss ways to use the Continuum of Self-Reflection and other tools to get to know individual teachers as people and as professionals, cultivating and fortifying the individual relationships that lead to effective performance. We investigate a talent-oriented and strength-based approach to leading and managing personnel. We set the stage for the collaborative work of creating and strengthening teams within the PLC framework, setting agreed-upon goals, and working toward achieving those goals.

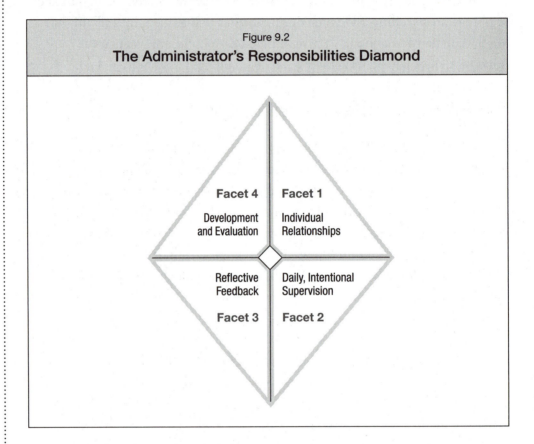

Figure 9.2
The Administrator's Responsibilities Diamond

Facet 2: Daily, Intentional Supervision

Chapter 11 includes the heart of the strength-based approach: a model of visiting classrooms that is known universally as the walk-through. Comparing our model of walk-throughs with a briefer version we call "rounds," we share ways to make this process individualized and intentional through the use of "look-fors" and the Continuum of Self-Reflection. We offer ideas for motivating, inspiring, and logging mini-observations in a meaningful, productive manner. This is the chapter that truly encourages administrators to focus on Quadrant II—and shows how to do it.

Facet 3: Reflective Feedback

Chapter 12 discusses the key elements of effective feedback. Filled with examples of directive comments, probing questions, and reflective feedback, it guides administrators through the process of coordinating the Continuum of Self-Reflection with the feedback we leave for teachers after conducting a walk-through for the purpose of encouraging reflective dialogue and continuous critical thinking.

Facet 4: Development and Evaluation

In Chapter 13, we discuss the various options that administrators have for designing professional development plans for each individual teacher on staff. Every teacher deserves a plan tailored to his or her professional needs as determined by individual goals, collaborative work, and baseline indicators on the Continuum of Self-Reflection. Along those lines, we debate the current form of "the teacher evaluation process" and discuss the ultimate goal of teacher evaluations. Can professional development goals and honest teacher appraisals coexist? We show you how to make this a reality.

Buckle Up!

School improvement is a serious business. The education of our youth is an investment in the future. The strategies and tactics you'll be reading about answer the noble and urgent call for immediate action in our discipline. This model of Strength-Based School Improvement, as implemented by the building administrator, is a powerful venture into the essential Quadrant II alcove in which improvement and growth reside. It is neither quick nor easy. It takes dedication, prioritization, and tremendous will. However, our schools deserve it. Our teachers deserve it. Our students deserve it. And the results yielded will benefit us all.

10

Individual Relationships

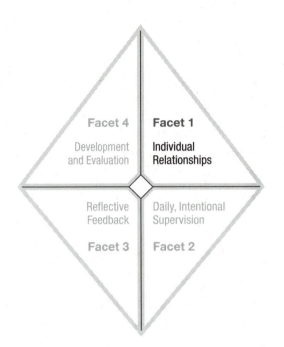

Facet 4
Development and Evaluation

Facet 1
Individual Relationships

Reflective Feedback

Daily, Intentional Supervision

Facet 3

Facet 2

One of the most beautiful and poetic aspects of an educator's job is that it involves working with people. Certainly there are folks out there who appreciate working with predictable and controllable machines—inanimate objects that they can pick up, put down, unplug, or program as necessary—and proceed throughout the course of their career without dealing with relationships, emotions, politics, behaviors, or the human element. Not so for us. We prefer the fun of dealing with people, in all their unique unpredictability.

Every teacher in your school is a unique and special individual—a compilation of strengths, weaknesses, talents, tendencies, skills, traits, characteristics, experiences, questions, attitudes, personalities, hopes, dreams, and thoughts. Think back to your first staff meeting at your current school, whether it was as an administrator, coach, or teacher. When you first met Mrs. Howdee, for example, you had no idea what was in store for you. You had no idea what this new person was really like, what drove her, or how well you two would work together (or even if you would get along).

Over time, you got to know Mrs. Howdee a little bit. Through conversations, observations (formal or informal), word around the school, and time spent working together, your knowledge of this teacher grew. You became much more aware of how to interact with her, what questions to ask, what topics to avoid, what her professional habits were, and what you could expect from her in the classroom.

This is a natural process, replacing curiosity and novelty with the understanding of reality.

For administrators, using the Strength-Based School Improvement approach means being dedicated to the pursuit of information about each individual teacher on staff. If you don't truly know the teachers, you cannot possibly hope to learn their strengths and maximize their potential. If you don't learn their strengths and maximize their potential, you have little chance of realizing significant school improvement. Phrased positively, if you, as an administrator, begin to understand your teachers on a higher level and cultivate a relationship with each as an individual, you can make intentional progress toward building every teacher's professional capacity. Thus, the time you spend gathering this information is critical and definitely worthwhile.

Marcus Buckingham and Curt Coffman, formerly with the Gallup Organization, conducted extensive research comprising interviews with more than 80,000 managers in over 400 companies to isolate what set the greatest managers apart from the rest. In their book *First, Break All the Rules*, they summarized their work with what could be the cornerstone of the Strength-Based School Improvement philosophy: "Despite their differences, great managers do share one thing: Before they do anything else, they first break all the rules of conventional wisdom. They consistently disregard the Golden Rule. And, yes, they even play favorites" (1999, p. 11).

That last sentence is one that always raises the hackles of educators, because for generations we've been trained in a vastly different mind-set. But remember, we're not herding cattle here. Differentiated leadership demands detailed insight into and an individual relationship with every follower under the leader's supervision. This is the first step—and the hardest step—and it is the one that generates the momentum to run the rest of this race. This is Facet 1 of the Administrator's Responsibilities Diamond.

A Strength-Based, Continuum-Guided Approach

What is the first thing you should do in order to get to know every individual teacher on staff? Observe them. Get out of the office; leave the e-mails, phone messages, and mailbox behind; and start logging steps on your pedometer. Watch your teachers in their own environment. Engage them in conversation, ask a lot of questions, and spend a good portion of the time listening. Talk about teaching. Talk about family. Talk about controversial subjects. Talk about their hopes and dreams—after all, these are your people, and "people are the most important resource at the school" (Harris, 2005, p. 172).

When working with people, we often overlook the fact that we all have our own idiosyncrasies and talents over which we may or may not have much control. As an effective administrator, you are responsible for seeking out, acknowledging, and understanding these innate characteristics—these strengths—that drive each staff member. Buckingham and Clifton (2001) wrote extensively about individuals' strengths in *Now, Discover Your Strengths*, detailing 34 "themes of talent" that people possess, with each theme defined as "a recurring pattern of thought, feeling, or behavior" (p. 79).

We highly recommend this book (and *First, Break All the Rules*) not only as a leadership guide but also as a tool to use with your entire teaching staff, perhaps in the form of a professional book club. There are shelves of leadership texts available for school administrators to read, and a good portion of them relate directly to education, but we have found none that addresses the issue of individual strengths as aptly and concisely as Buckingham's business-based books do. As a follow-up to a whole-staff (or grade-level team, or department, or any other staff configuration) book club, we suggest that every teacher complete the StrengthsFinder Profile (available at www.strengthsfinder.com) to discover his or her five most dominant strengths. (A code included in each copy of *First, Break All the Rules* gives the book's owner access to the profile.) There are literally dozens of accessible personality-type and self-awareness surveys that could aid us in the pursuit of self-discovery, and each has its own merit and could probably generate meaningful reflective discussions, but the Gallup Organization, which operates the Web site on which the StrengthsFinder Profile is located, is without peer when it comes to asking the right questions and uncovering the appropriate information.

Uncovering the information is the goal here. Discovering and discussing each teacher's unique "themes of talent" will help you get to know him or her in a way that you may not have considered before. What's more, when these same teachers engage in the critical art of self-reflection as they predict their strengths, evaluate the accuracy of the StrengthsFinder Profile, and consider the implications of their strengths on their daily work, they are addressing a primary focus of the Strength-Based philosophy.

Here we begin to merge the Continuum of Self-Reflection with the savvy administrator's investigation of individual strengths and talents. In which stage of the Continuum does Mrs. Howdee land? How do her innate strengths relate to that stage? Do her strength-based conversations indicate accurate and insightful self-reflection? Do other teachers with similar self-reflective tendencies reveal strengths similar to Mrs. Howdee's? What are the differences? To what factors can you attribute those differences?

Even without reviewing the reports of each teacher's themes of talent, you can collect loads of information about the teacher through observations, both formal classroom ones and informal, around-the-water-cooler ones. We suggest compiling notes, anecdotes, and other data to help place each teacher on the Continuum of Self-Reflection. Watch. Listen. Notice. Those data, as part of a bigger collection of teacher information, will help you as you work toward differentiating the supervision process.

A by-product of this process is that, armed with this information about each staff member, you may well find out if you have followed Jim Collins's advice in *Good to Great* to "get the right people on the bus" and "get them in the right seats" (2001, p. 41). There are certain positions within a school that require people with specific strengths. There are also some strengths that may preclude a person's effectiveness in particular jobs. You would be remiss as a school administrator to be unaware of these mismatches and fail to act on them.

Pete's Perspective

When we hired "Mr. Nahunu," an extremely dedicated and sharp young man, to teach 1st grade, he expressed his desire to instill a love of school and an appreciation for "critical literacy" in the 6-year-olds over whom he would watch. His references from his previous school, where he had taught 3rd grade for a couple of years, were positive. Everything seemed to be in order; Mr. Nahunu looked to be a perfect fit to tackle the challenge of teaching 1st grade in our school. Or so we thought.

Unfortunately, a year or so into the new assignment, we realized he wasn't really enjoying the work. Mr. Nahunu knew the ins and outs of good instruction, could recite the latest research on best practices, and was a highly reflective, intelligent individual. However, he had a devil of a time building strong, enduring relationships with his students, and without those bonds, student motivation and classroom management were a struggle. In his daily work, Mr. Nahunu exhibited the strengths of *intellection* and *learner,* meaning he had a tremendous need to think and to learn (Buckingham & Clifton, 2001). The 1st grade curriculum and relatively low level of intellectual conversation he had with his students had drained him of his enthusiasm.

As fortune would have it, eventually the correct plan for Mr. Nahunu fell into place, and we were able to transfer him into a 5th grade classroom. A different teacher emerged. With the older, more mature students he could share deeper conversations, engaging them in Socratic arguments that challenged everyone in the room to think at a different level. His class came together as a community, and Mr. Nahunu's classroom management issues disappeared. It turned out to be a perfect fit for him and for us, but without that understanding of his innate characteristics, we may have continued to push Mr. Nahunu in a role for which he was not designed.

Goal Setting

Once you have acquired some meaningful information about each individual teacher, you must chart a plan to develop each person's skills, influence, and capacity. This challenge opens a whole new can of worms. How do you identify what a teacher needs to work on? How can you accurately link a teacher's personal strengths with his or her classroom responsibilities? The goal-setting step is critical to the success of Strength-Based School Improvement.

Teachers in different stages along the Continuum of Self-Reflection will require different types of goals, as well as various amounts of guidance in the goal-setting process. Let's proceed now through an overview of the parameters of goal setting by administrators and teachers stage by stage.

Unaware-Stage Teachers

Teachers in the Unaware stage will likely need the administrator to take a more directive approach. Since they often exhibit little or no knowledge of best practices, it is up to the administrator to provide that area of focus. Also, since they typically work in isolation from their teammates, teachers in this stage would benefit from a team goal, one previously established by grade-level or subject-area colleagues, or one closely linked to it. This may be in lieu of an individual goal. Unaware teachers will benefit from having support, encouragement, and time with partners, as well as from being able to see what their colleagues are doing and how they are doing it. A collaborative goal set with the entire team is a perfect way to do just that.

Conscious-Stage Teachers

Teachers in the Conscious stage will generally respond best to an administrator who coaxes a particular goal out of them. Typically knowledgeable but inconsistent, they are capable of following the administrator's train of thought to its intended destination. Conscious teachers will hear an administrator's pointed compliments ("You have a real strength for teaching listening comprehension skills") and questions ("Have you considered how that matches up with the students' independent reading comprehension abilities?") and translate them into the realization that "Yes, this area is important and an area that I could certainly improve; this is something I'd like to work on as an individual goal." A key for goal setting with teachers in the Conscious stage is to keep the goal very specific. The details ensure accountability, which is one of the obstacles these teachers typically face.

Action-Stage Teachers

Teachers in the Action stage are motivated to apply their knowledge with more consistency. With that in mind, the administrator must simply ensure that the teacher-selected goals match what they are actually working on in the classroom. Action teachers need support in learning how to refine their work. The administrator is responsible for establishing a big-picture goal and providing a proper balance of the leeway for the teacher to try out new strategies and requiring the accountability of specific, results-driven feedback. Action teachers need to know how their new strategies have paid off in pursuit of the goal.

Refinement-Stage Teachers

Teachers in the Refinement stage can set whatever goal they want, because the overwhelming odds are that the goal will be appropriate and meaningful and that they will defy hell and high water to find a way to achieve it. Highly self-reflective and inherently responsive, Refinement teachers are already constantly on the lookout for a better mousetrap. The administrator's responsibilities in goal setting for the Refinement-stage teacher are to listen, record teachers' thoughts, and pledge support. Often, these teachers show a surprising lack of focus, offering an opportunity for the administrator to synthesize teachers' endeavors and propose a new challenge that is related to the teachers' strengths.

Making Goals SMART

All goals, regardless of other factors, must share some common characteristics, embodied in the SMART acronym, which many educators are familiar with and can probably recite:

• *Specific.* This helps all parties know exactly what they're talking about, avoiding confusion and the unfortunate circumstances that surround communication breakdowns.

• *Measurable.* It sounds obvious, but if the goal doesn't include a tangible measurement of some kind, how could anyone possibly know if it's been reached?

• *Attainable.* Every goal has to be within the sphere of the possible, an objective that, with proper support and effort, is within reach.

• *Results-oriented.* Rather than emphasize a process, effective goals focus on the end result. What is it the teacher truly expects to accomplish?

• *Time-bound.* When establishing a time frame for a goal, it must be realistic but also aggressive. This helps keep a healthy level of anxiety and focus on the goal.

When setting goals, everyone involved should be focused on multiple types of evidence: of learning, of improvement, of growth, and of impact. Regardless of who has the most influence in setting the goals, or even what steps are included, the premium is on the outcomes. The days of "cardiac assessments"—"I feel in my heart that the adjustments I made helped these children"—are over. We need proof that our interventions yielded dividends. It has been said that what gets measured gets done. Figure 10.1 shows a filled-in version of a form we have used to collect appropriate evidence.

Figure 10.1

Sample SMART Goal-Setting Form for Teachers

Teacher Name: Mrs. Duncan   **Today's Date:** 9/4

Goal (specific and measurable):
90% of the students in Mrs. Duncan's class (and in 3rd grade overall) will pass each mathematics end-of-unit test

Baseline data (specific and measurable):
Pre-assessment scores for each end-of-unit test assessing the students' understanding of the same standards but in a slightly different format

Timeline:
• Projected end-of-1st-unit test: 10/19
• Check-in dates: 9/14, 9/21, 9/28, 10/5, 10/12

Evidence (results) of effectiveness:
• *Passing* is defined as demonstrating mastery of 80% or more of the standards measured on each end-of-unit test
• *Mastery* is defined as scoring 1/1 or 2/2 points on the applicable question on each end-of-unit test

Strategies to employ:
• Teacher will use self-created pre-assessments
• Teacher will employ ongoing formative assessments (homework, quizzes, work samples, etc.)
• Teacher will implement ongoing intervention sessions, including before-school "cram" classes and individualized (or small-group) instruction during centers
• Teacher will identify and emphasize the standards that students are expected to learn
• Teacher will match standards with the instruction

Resources available to attain the goal:
• Additional instructional staff (paraprofessional, Title I teacher, resource teacher)
• Math "investigations" materials
• Pre-tests generated by 3rd grade team last year
• Instructional coach will model lessons as requested
• Substitute funds are available to bring in a sub so that the teacher can finish assessments or observe colleagues within the building

Putting PLCs to Work

Bountiful research supports the creation and cultivation of professional learning communities (DuFour & Eaker, 1998; Marzano, 2003; McKeever, 2003; Schmoker, 2006). If you have already established your school as a PLC, you've got a ton of supports in place. The teachers are members of pertinent teams. How, then, do they determine a team (grade-level, subject-area) goal? It's important to mention that teachers in every stage of the Continuum of Self-Reflection, from Unaware to Refinement, can benefit from the support and input of their teammates. This speaks to high levels of accountability, motivation, interdependence, and collaboration.

First, set team goals for every team. The goal-setting meeting should include anyone who has anything to do with that particular team and its students, in particular support staff, instructional paraprofessionals, coaches, and resource teachers. It is not uncommon for multiple teams within the same building to have very similar goals, especially if the school's vision is clear and compelling to all stakeholders. These goals should be SMART goals, and they should relate directly to the most important work that team could engage in.

Next, identify the people for whom the team goal is enough. Generally speaking, for some of the teachers in every building (such as those in the Unaware stage), a team goal is enough to keep them focused. An additional individual goal might distract their attention or might just pull them in another direction enough to compromise both goals. Thus, since the team goal in the PLC format will provide team accountability, offer built-in support mechanisms, and encourage collaboration, it's a perfect place to spend a lot of energy and make potentially huge gains.

Finally, set individual goals with the rest of the team members. Consider their strengths, their current placement on the Continuum, their team goal, and their assignment when setting individual goals.

The success of the goal-setting process hinges on your willingness to listen, observe, and learn as much as you can about every individual teacher, followed by the uncompromising dedication to act accordingly. The more administrators know about their people, and the stronger their interpersonal and professional relationships with them are, the tighter the alignment between the school's needs and its goals. The more energy you frontload into learning about your teachers, the stronger and more effective your teams will be, and the more growth your entire school will realize.

11

Daily, Intentional Supervision

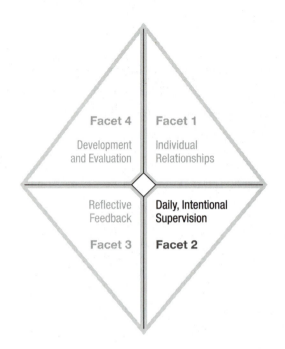

Facet 4
Development and Evaluation

Facet 1
Individual Relationships

Reflective Feedback

Daily, Intentional Supervision

Facet 3

Facet 2

After you have established individual and team goals for each teacher in the building, it's time to turn your attention to the next facet of an administrator's responsibilities under Strength-Based School Improvement: daily, intentional supervision. This supervision takes place via two primary means: *rounds* and *walk-throughs*. You may have heard of walk-throughs, and maybe you've even been trained in one model or another of "the walk-through process," but our version is a bit different. As you will read later in this chapter, the Hall Walk-Through (for lack of a better name, as it has been modified and adapted by author Pete Hall) is distinguished from other models because it contains two novel concepts: (1) immediate, intentional, written feedback that guides teachers' reflective practice and (2) a dual utility for developmental and evaluative purposes.

For administrators, practicing daily, intentional supervision reaps astonishingly broad and deep benefits. First, as administrators spend more time in classrooms, the quality and strength of adult–adult (and adult–child) relationships around the building increase. Opportunities to observe authentic professional practice abound. Teachers appreciate having the administrator actively involved in the educational and professional growth process. Students learn about the administrator as a person, and the mystique that accompanies the "voice from the PA system" or "face on the video monitor" is replaced by the recognition of another responsible adult around campus. We contend that the real work of school administrators is not done in the office, at a desk, in front of a computer. Rather, it's done where the action is: where the students are learning and where the teachers are teaching—in the classrooms, in the hallways, and in the supply closets that have been converted into teaching nooks.

Astoundingly, the majority of school-based administrators still perform roughly 95 percent of their daily work in places other than the school's classrooms. We all know administrators who are wrapped up in meetings, locked in the office, and buried by paperwork. If any one of us were to refer back to Chapter 9, compare a list of what we typically *do* as administrators versus what we know we *should* be doing, and assign all of those activities to a quadrant in Covey's Time Management Matrix, we might well be embarrassed by our misguided focus.

Mike Schmoker (2006) exhorts administrators to have the "courage to monitor" classroom instruction and teams' progress toward their curricular goals (p. 129). Intentionally and repeatedly monitoring teacher behaviors, right there in the middle of the classroom battlefield, is not for the faint of heart. It takes more than the courage Schmoker urges; it takes stout dedication, immense self-discipline, and an unyielding belief that your involvement will eventually result in teacher growth and increased student learning.

The Devil Is in the Details

In the great scheme of things, supervising teachers with frequency and intentionality is one of the "high-leverage" activities Marshall (2006) espouses as essential to success. And he's not alone in his support. A little more than a decade ago, in *Differentiated Supervision*, Allan Glatthorn (1997) discussed the need for administrators to conduct frequent, informal classroom visits and the benefits thereof. Master research-synthesizer and author Robert J. Marzano compiled a list of the top 21 responsibilities of the school administrator in *School Leadership That Works* (Marzano, Waters, & McNulty, 2005) and found that monitoring the effectiveness of school practices had the third-highest correlation to student academic achievement of the bunch—trailing only situational effectiveness and flexibility, which might be more readily described as *characteristics* than as *behaviors*.

We find one of Marcus Buckingham's revelations amusingly accurate. In discussing the influence (or lack thereof) of a manager who isn't actively supervising employees, Buckingham and Coffman (1999) wrote, "All you can do is influence, motivate, berate, or cajole in the hope that most of your people will do what you ask of them. This isn't control. It's remote control" (p. 109). Buckingham followed up in *The One Thing You Need to Know . . . About Great Managing, Great Leading, and Sustained Individual Success* with this clear-cut directive: "Get out of your office and observe" (2005, p. 124).

In the end, Stephen Covey would be proud of any administrators who dedicate significant time to these Quadrant II efforts despite all the tugs and pulls from the other quadrants attempting to derail us from our mission. In his study titled *What Great Principals Do Differently*, Todd Whitaker (2003) concluded, "Great [administrators] have an equal number of demands placed on their time. They just do not let these reasons keep them from doing what matters most: improving teacher effectiveness in their schools" (p. 37). So how do you do that? By attending to Facet 2 of administrative duties: daily, intentional supervision.

Rounds

Imagine a hospital floor with 14 patients. When it's time for "rounds," the physician assigned to these patients visits each room to check on each patient individually. She walks in, grabs the chart, and scans the test results, EKG readings, nurse's notes, and other pertinent information. She may talk to the nurse on duty about recent changes in the patient's condition. Then, if the patient is awake, she engages in a quick conversation to gauge what sort of progress the patient is making, where the pain is, and if there are any changes that she should know about. It's not a lengthy interview; rather, it's a few focused minutes that tell the doctor if this patient is on the right path to recovery. In short order, she's on to the next patient.

Our educational version of rounds is very similar. The administrator enters each classroom, scans the immediate events ("checks the chart"), and moves on to the next classroom. It's not a lengthy process; rather, it's a brief, focused window that tells the administrator if everything is proceeding as planned in that classroom. And when we say "brief," we mean it. A single visit to one classroom should last no longer than 30 to 45 seconds.

During rounds, the administrator seldom communicates directly with the teacher or the students. The administrator provides no immediate feedback, poses no questions, and does not interrupt the lesson itself. Instead, these quick observations are a means of gathering data that indicate trends, exemplify strengths, reveal areas of concern, and uncover tendencies. There may be time later to discuss observations and to engage a teacher in a conversation, but for now the administrator is simply looking at big-picture elements, gauging the forest instead of the trees.

During that brief 30- to 45-second visit, the administrator's attention should be focused on what we have come to call "the Big Four":

1. *Instructional strategy.* It does not take much time to determine whether the teacher is lecturing or circulating the classroom during independent work time, what type of questioning strategy the teacher is using, or if the teacher is activating the students' prior knowledge. The administrator basically asks, "What is the teacher doing?"

2. *Student engagement.* The students' orientation to the teacher or to the learning objective is immediately obvious when one enters a classroom. The extent to which the students are demonstrating a skill, attending to a project, or working in concert with each other answers the question, "What are the students doing?"

3. *Curricular adherence.* Identifying whether the teacher is following the adopted district curriculum is a tad more complicated, but only if the administrator is unfamiliar with the district curriculum. The administrator must ask, "Are the students learning or practicing something that will help them master their grade-level standards?"

4. *Classroom management.* As Pete Hall's mentor and colleague Frank Garrity used to say, "You've got to get the kids in the learning mode first." It should not take more than 15 seconds to determine if the students are in the "learning mode" (paying attention, on task, behaving appropriately, and ready to work) and if the classroom is under control. Fortunately, the answer to this challenge lies at the end of a question the administrator will already have asked: "What are the students doing?"

A Goal for Rounds

If each classroom visit during rounds lasts only between 30 to 45 seconds, a complete circuit of a 24-classroom campus should take you roughly 15 minutes. This is a pretty moderate investment of time, especially when you consider that this task falls into Covey's Quadrant II and is among the most meaningful work you can engage in during a typical day. Our goal for daily rounds is two circuits, daily, which means getting into each classroom twice a day for a total of one or two minutes. This requires just about a half an hour each day. Of course, the size of the school and teaching staff will factor into how much time it will take you to complete meaningful rounds—but we say, the higher the aim, the better!

Walk-Throughs: The Ultimate Tool for Administrators

Sticking with the medical analogy, the Hall Walk-Through is like a physical examination. It may not include the full panel of blood tests and an MRI, but it's the equivalent of entering each classroom with a stethoscope, blood pressure gauge, and tongue depressor: checking things out in detail and having a critical look around.

Over the years, especially in the past decade or so, different walk-through models have cropped up in the education landscape. Many school districts, universities, and programs tout one version of the walk-through technique or another, and each has its own advantages. From *School Management by Wandering Around* (Frase & Hetzel, 1990) to *Cognitive Coaching* (Costa & Garmston, 1994), and from the University of Pittsburgh's team walk-through model (Werlinich, 2003) to Downey's three-minute walk-through (Downey, Steffy, English, Frase, & Poston, 2004) and a host of others, the methodology and definition of the term have been soaked and wrung out more times than a bathtub washcloth.

Even administrators who are using identical terminology may not be sure they're speaking the same language. *Walk-throughs. Learning walks. Touring the castle. Management by wandering around.* It's a dizzying array of terms and definitions. So how is the Hall Walk-Through different and noteworthy?

Geared to serve multiple purposes in a short, simple, and replicable format, the Hall Walk-Through process is firmly entrenched in the strength-based philosophy. Effectively used, it provides administrators with ample opportunities to see authentic instruction, unscripted classroom interactions, and unadulterated learning. In short, you get to see what's really going on in the classrooms.

The Hall Walk-Through starts with the administrator entering a classroom unobtrusively and finding a place to sit or perch to observe the classroom. Over the course of the next 5 to 15 minutes (the time varies depending on the lesson, the teacher, and the learning objective, among other variables), the administrator will carefully observe the teacher and students. While the Big Four concepts (instructional strategy, student engagement, curricular adherence, and classroom management) certainly come into play, this mini-observation is really quite focused on a particular area of emphasis—which we call a "look-for." At the end of the classroom observation, the administrator writes a brief, intentional, feedback-focused note on the Hall Walk-Through Reflection Form (see Figure 11.1) and leaves a copy on the teacher's desk on the way out the door. Then the administrator proceeds to the next classroom.

A Goal for Walk-Throughs

Staying with Covey's Quadrant II as much as possible, our goal for walk-throughs is modest: intentional walk-through visits of three to five different classrooms per day. Since each classroom "mini-observation" lasts anywhere from 5 to 15 minutes, the total daily investment should land in the 45- to 75-minute range. This is enough to provide each teacher with specific feedback on a regular basis (depending on the size of the school, it could be once a week or every other week). Coupled with rounds, the process will give the administrator a pretty comprehensive picture of the current status of teaching and learning throughout the school.

"Unobtrusivity"

Teachers and students have various responses to an administrator's presence in the classroom. Some are compelled to stop what they're doing and formally announce the visitor's arrival. Others wave and say hi, or announce exactly what they are doing right then. As Downey and colleagues (2004) explained, "Students

Figure 11.1
The Hall Walk-Through Reflection Form

DOWNLOAD

Teacher: _____ Date: _____ Time: _____

Content: _____

Look-For Focus: _____

What is the TEACHER doing?

_____

_____

_____

_____

What are STUDENTS doing?

_____

_____

_____

_____

Comments: _____

_____

_____

_____

_____

_____

_____

_____

are experts at knowing how to engage their visitors so they do not have to do their work" (p. 22). Ideally, when a site administrator walks into a classroom, the teacher and the students should continue to do exactly what they were doing prior to the administrator's arrival. Of course, both teachers and students will need to be trained to "ignore" the arrival so that the administrator can get the most authentic view of the classroom goings-on. And the administrator must practice "unobtrusivity" and not cause a scene.

Achieving this goal takes some time and repetitive practice. The administrator needs to tell the staff: "Keep teaching. Keep conferencing with that student. Keep administering that quiz. The only thing that just changed is that I became a quasi-camouflaged part of the classroom scenery." These instructions should be communicated in the staff meetings and team collaboration sessions that precede the school year, when the administrator sets the foundation for classroom visits, walk-throughs, and the evaluation process. For students, the message is the same: "When I come in the room, I want to see you working. I want to notice how intelligent and well-behaved you are. If you want to give me one little wave and a smile, that's OK, but then get back to work! Pretend I'm not even here." Eventually, after plenty of reminders (to students and teachers alike), you'll be able to slide right in and observe each classroom "in the wild."

Look-Fors

As mentioned earlier, the Hall Walk-Through includes a targeted area of emphasis, better known as a "look-for"—a clear outline of what the administrator hopes or expects to see. Whereas other versions of walk-throughs send administrators into classrooms without direction or provide detailed steps that may or may not match the teacher's (or students') needs (Downey et al., 2004; Glatthorn, 1997), the Hall Walk-Through's initial effectiveness is born of the classroom visit having a specified purpose, which the administrator notes on the "Look-For Focus" line of the checklist (see Figure 11.1). The administrator has a direction.

There is a method to the madness, though the concept brings up a couple of valid questions.

Where do the look-fors come from? Useful look-fors stem from intentional, focused discussions between the administrator and the teacher or teachers in question. Sometimes the entire school staff will agree on a certain look-for because it fits into the current focus of the schoolwide improvement plan. Look-fors can also come from a grade-level team's goal, especially if the goal lends itself to a particular instructional strategy. Individual teachers could have differentiated look-fors related to their own goals and expertise.

A key to determining effective look-fors is to keep the entire process transparent—every teacher on staff should know exactly what the look-fors are and what effective practice would look like when observed so that there is no confusion or misunderstanding throughout the process. In short, when the administrator walks into the room, the teacher should already know what the administrator expects to observe.

What does an effective look-for look like? Here are several solid examples:

- *Schoolwide*
  —The administrator expects to see all teachers explicitly teaching the learning objectives for every lesson.
  —The administrator expects to note all teachers using positive language when interacting with the children.

- *Grade-level*
  —The administrator expects to observe all 2nd grade teachers using interactive writing strategies across the curriculum.
  —The administrator expects to notice all 8th grade teachers providing math instruction in groupings that match the results of the pre-assessment data.

- *Individual*
  —The administrator expects to see Mrs. Francois implementing a more patient approach with intentional wait time.
  —The administrator expects to see Mr. Ellsbury requesting that students take a more active role in their own education by explaining their thinking to the rest of the class.

Feedback

We'll dive deeper into the feedback discussion in Chapter 12's look at Facet 3 of an administrator's responsibilities, but suffice it to say that feedback is one element that makes the Hall Walk-Through model so different and so effective. With this walk-through method, the administrator leaves some sort of feedback—in particular, written feedback—for the classroom teacher after every visit. This approach stands in stark contrast to the occasional conversation that follows typical classroom walk-throughs (Downey et al., 2004; Marshall, 2005), the overkill of comprehensive scripted feedback that accompanies the clinical evaluation model (Danielson & McGreal, 2000; Glatthorn, 1997), and the glaring absence of feedback from the bulk of school administrators who either do not visit classrooms on a regular basis or meander from room to room without a meaningful direction.

This precise, immediate feedback is written down and left for the teacher when the administrator exits the classroom. Whether or not the administrator and teacher have an opportunity later to exchange dialogue regarding the contents, teachers always have something to banter about with colleagues, consider in silent self-reflection, or rant about to their spouses!

Formative vs. Summative Uses of Observational Data

The second major difference between the Hall Walk-Through and all the other variations out there is its role in the evaluation of instructional staff. The Hall Walk-Through is an observational tool designed to encourage self-reflection, build teacher capacity, and aid in the teacher evaluation process. As we discussed in Chapter 2, the school administrator should serve as a continuous evaluator. An administrator needs to keep an eye on every aspect of the school to make sure that everything within the school is running smoothly; naturally, classroom observations provide an ideal opportunity for evaluating what is happening in the classroom.

In what we consider a bizarre turn of events, here in the United States, administrator walk-throughs are often exempt from consideration as evaluative tools. The language of negotiated contracts, the perception of capricious administrator behavior, and the dangerous precedent of pretending these walk-throughs didn't really exist preclude observations made during walk-through visits from becoming a part of teachers' annual performance reviews. Even walk-through proponent Glatthorn (1997) emphasizes that these frequent, informal visits "should not be used in the formal teacher evaluation system" (p. 20).

As part of our discussion of Facet 4 in Chapter 12, we rebuke these outdated and precarious conditions as we further investigate the many uses of the Hall Walk-Through process for both formative and summative purposes.

Making It Happen

For the vast majority of school administrators, the idea of implementing rounds and walk-throughs is more grandiose and lofty than realistic and practical. The real-life complications brought about by scheduling conflicts, paperwork demands, teachers union outcries, testing requirements, budgeting challenges, discipline investigations, legal issues, and countless other Quadrant III factors threaten to strip even the most positive and committed administrators of their personal energy and resolve. Daily, intentional supervision often gets lost in the shuffle.

Fortunately, we have created, adapted, and refined a method we believe will help even the most overwhelmed, frantic administrators find the resolve necessary to undertake these essential, high-leverage activities. It all boils down to a couple of key understandings.

You must prioritize your actions. The first step in reclaiming your own administratorship is to "quadrantize your work" (Hall, 2006b), keeping your focus on activities that fall into Quadrant II of Covey's Time Management Matrix. If you were to engage in the reflective practice of assigning tasks to Covey's quadrants as they come across your desk, you will quickly realize that activities that fall into Quadrant III (routine business) and Quadrant IV (handoffs) are draining your time and energy immensely. Flip back to Chapter 9 to review a more detailed explanation of prioritization strategies.

You must find your own "hook" to stay motivated. There are many from which to choose:

• *Intrinsic motivation.* For some of us, the motivation to succeed and excel, or at least to implement a best practice, comes from within. Such intrinsic motivation is helpful but rare, and many find it difficult to maintain for extended periods of time.

• *Goal setting.* Others need a written (SMART) goal to help hone their focus. We have established reasonable starting goals for rounds (twice into each classroom per day) and walk-throughs (three to five classroom visits per day), though certainly that will vary from school to school and administrator to administrator.

• *Accountability.* Sharing your goals with the teaching staff may help to keep you actively focused on your priorities. Teachers' expectations of seeing you in their classrooms and requests for your presence can provide a powerful incentive.

• *Competition.* Some administrators find that a little friendly (or feisty) competition is what it takes to hold our feet to the fire. If this is you, challenge another administrator to record the number of walk-throughs you perform and put a Saturday lunch on the wager.

• *Logging.* If lists and tally marks occupy the sticky notes plastered all over your office desk, then you are a candidate for maintaining a log of walk-through visits, which might range from a journal-style record of each walk-through to a simple list of teacher names and walk-through dates to an even simpler calendar where you record the initials of the teachers whose classrooms you walk-through each day.

Pete's Perspective

I am a logger. I don't mean that I enjoy cutting down trees or clear-cutting mountain ranges; I mean, I'm one of those people who make lists with little boxes next to each item. Nothing gives me more joy than completing tasks and checking off the boxes on my lists.

OK, that was an exaggeration, but the truth is I maintain logs of many elements of my life. At home, I monitor our finances with a detailed budget spreadsheet and keep a log of my personal workout regimen. Without them, I fear I might slip into laziness or lose the momentum I gather from the success of completion. For me, it works.

At school, the same rings true. I have lists on sticky notes plastered all over my desk. And for keeping track of my rounds and walk-throughs? You guessed it: a manila folder with a hand-crafted chart, replete with daily tally marks, weekly totals, and a monthly graph.

I do this not because anyone else will ever look at it (chances are, no one will). Rather, it's for myself. I set daily, weekly, and monthly goals, and I strive to attain them. The logs and charts help me assess my progress along the way and ensure that I'm making visits to each teacher's classroom with the requisite frequency.

Often, I review the logs to see how I can modify my behaviors to better meet my goals. For instance, one year I conducted 362 walk-through visits. That might seem like a lot, but it's an average of only two per day. There were days in which I made zero classroom visits. It stung me to write the "0" on my logs those days, and I spent my commute home considering how much time I actually had spent engaged in Quadrant II activities. What would Covey say about my day? Had I effectively prioritized my work?

The most helpful advice I can offer is this: *Know yourself.* Only you know what will work to keep you plugging away, and you may find yourself attempting various strategies to discover which one works. Despite all my efforts, I have been utterly unable to get my son to embrace the practice of logging. I'm not sure if it's just teenage rebellion, but he's managed to ignore all my pleas to log his own soccer work-outs, maintain a list of upcoming school assignments, or record the extra chores he's completed around the house. It turns out, however, he's just figuring out his own way to stay motivated and stay connected.

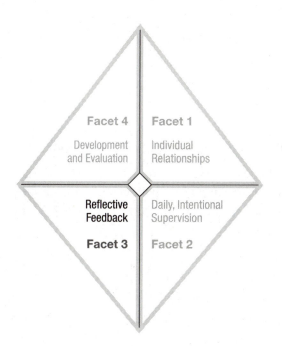

Facet 4
Development
and Evaluation

Facet 1
Individual
Relationships

**Reflective
Feedback**

Daily, Intentional
Supervision

Facet 3

Facet 2

12

Reflective Feedback

Now that we have established that effective administrators are in classrooms as often as possible and have created a realistic plan for making this happen, it's time to focus on what we expect to occur during this time. What is the end result you, as an administrator, should be aiming for? What is the ultimate goal?

Clearly, you're interested in improving student achievement by increasing each teacher's capacity for success. The path that you are attempting to usher each teacher down, however, is not simply one of refined skills and improved strategies. Rather, this path is one of introspection, focused on the critical analysis of one's own teaching practices, decision making, and thinking processes. Administrators aim to guide each individual teacher along the Continuum of Self-Reflection, with the ultimate goal of encouraging long-term professional growth and continuous, accurate self-reflection.

From the administrator's point of view, conducting frequent rounds and walk-throughs is a terrific start. A step into the classroom is a huge step in the right direction. However, just getting into the classrooms on a regular basis won't accomplish that by itself, just as opening the hood of your car and looking inside won't make it run more smoothly. Improvement requires action. And what is the action you must take to make walk-throughs the effective professional growth tools they can be? You must provide reflective feedback.

Feedback is the critical element that further distinguishes this model of walk-throughs from all the other models out there. Some models focus on feedback that provides generic benefits to the group, rather than emphasizing the unique developmental needs of individual teachers. Carolyn Downey and her team introduced a solid model with *The Three-Minute Classroom Walk-Through* (Downey et al., 2004), though it offers a structure more beneficial to the administrator than each teacher. Still other models (Werlinich, 2003, for example) espouse the benefits of group debriefing with an eye on systemic growth. Where our model differs is in the immediacy, specificity, and reliability of feedback directed to the individual teacher level that is intended to compel the teacher to reflect and grow as a professional. This reflective feedback is the crux of Facet 3 of the Administrator's Responsibilities Diamond.

Through the Looking Glass

We have stated over and over that the primary purpose of an administrator's work is to increase the capacity of each individual teacher on staff, just as the teacher's role is to increase the knowledge and skill of each individual student in the classroom. We have established that there is a dangerously widespread lack of transfer between the research-based instructional "best practices" and the instruction delivered by the majority of teachers in classrooms today. Why does this gap persist? What factors mitigate administrators' valiant attempts to implement the most recent, tried-and-true instructional methods available? Why, for instance, can't you take your extensive knowledge and leverage it to bring about stellar classroom teaching in every classroom? What are the complicating variables?

A systematic, strategic approach to providing feedback to teachers will help you traverse this chasm. For years, teachers have known that an effective way to individualize classroom instruction is to provide informative feedback to the students, one child at a time. Research definitively supports the proposal that feedback can act as an accelerant to learning (Danielson, 2007; Marzano, Pickering, & Pollock, 2001; Reeves, 2006; Stiggins, 2004b).

Here is a scenario that ought to drive the point home. Two students in a 7th grade science class, both of whom understood the learning objective in a particular lesson, worked diligently on individual projects designed to demonstrate their mastery of the material. Neither project was up to par, according to the teacher. She recorded a grade of *D* for both projects, but gave the students one week to improve their work and resubmit it for a higher mark. The teacher provided one student with detailed feedback and explained where improvements could be made. The other student received no feedback whatsoever. Which student is more likely to demonstrate increased learning as a result of this experience? Clearly, the one who received feedback will be better prepared and more likely to gain from the second opportunity, because that student will have more precise tools to use for improvement.

The idea is the same for an administrator's work with teachers. If you get into each classroom every day via rounds and walk-throughs, you have the opportunity to observe teaching "in the wild," experiencing it in as authentic a manner as possible. What tremendous possibility lies in wait for the savvy administrator who is truly seeking an arena to engage teachers in critical thought, self-reflection, and open inquiry in order to strengthen teaching practices! All of this can happen within the confines of a series of 5- to 15-minute walk-throughs—but only if you provide effective feedback.

Let's take a moment to define the term *effective*. Simply put, feedback is effective if it helps the teacher to improve in knowledge, skill, or self-reflective behavior. Buckingham and Coffman (1999) emphasize that great leaders excel at "holding up the mirror" for their employees. Great administrators offer their teachers the professional favor of giving them direct performance feedback, allowing them the opportunity to take that feedback and implement a strategy to address a concern, identify a strength, rectify an error, consider an alternative, and, in the end, improve their future performance. In order for this to happen and feedback to be effective, it must contain certain characteristics. We sum these up using the acronym TARP.

Covering It with TARP

The administrator's feedback must first of all be *timely*. By "timely," we mean "immediate" as opposed to "delayed"—and immediacy is the single most important characteristic of effective feedback. Researchers from Pennsylvania State University said, "The target for feedback timing should be as close to the instructional event as possible" (Scheeler, Ruhl, & McAfee, 2004), meaning during the lesson, immediately following the lesson, or at least within the same half-day window. Clearly, interrupting a classroom lesson to provide oral feedback to the teacher directly might cause more harm to the lesson itself than good to the teacher's long-term growth. But waiting until the teacher has the opportunity to come to the office to chat, uninterrupted, with the administrator might involve a delay of several days, if not weeks! The Hall Walk-Through Reflection Form (see Figure 11.1, p. 130) eliminates the guesswork and provides a simple venue for providing written feedback directly to the teacher that can be read immediately following the administrator's departure or at the teacher's leisure.

Second, the feedback must be *accurate*. If it isn't accurate, it's not worth sharing. This is a critical piece of the puzzle, and this is where the administrator's role as "instructional leader" must be solidified, credible, and respected. Teachers require and demand feedback that is technically correct, worthwhile, and precise. These are the same criteria that we ask teachers to provide to students (Reeves, 2006). In just a moment, we will address specificity in feedback further.

Third, the feedback must be *relevant* with regard to the teacher's goals—the individual objective, the grade-level or team goal, and/or the schoolwide focus. Feedback that matches one or all of these criteria is likely to be embraced more readily, considered more carefully, and more apt to be put into use. This is also the basis behind using look-fors to keep us focused—they keep our eyes on the prize (Downey et al., 2004).

Finally, the feedback must be *private*. Even though educators (like us, for example!) espouse the need to work collaboratively and in teams, the benefits of delivering private feedback, directly to individual teachers, are clear. This solidifies the notion that the relationship between administrator and teacher is of the utmost importance. As the administrator's responsibility here is to help each individual teacher improve and meet his or her potential, it's not a stretch to suggest that the administrator provide effective feedback to the teacher directly, in a confidential, trust-building manner. Buckingham and Coffman (1999) suggest giving feedback one on one, especially if it might be construed as negative or less than flattering. That said, as teachers become comfortable with the process, many will eventually share the feedback they receive with each other, asking fellow teachers for additional thoughts, clarifications, and suggestions. Colleagues discussing feedback in a collaborative arena multiplies the effect of the feedback itself, offers further opportunities for teachers to engage in professional discourse, and amplifies the likelihood that the feedback will be put to good use.

Other Feedback Considerations

An additional quality of effective feedback is its continuousness. When teachers receive feedback once or twice a year (as is typical under the overly relied-upon clinical evaluation model), it is generally overwhelmingly comprehensive and untimely, rendering it virtually useless for application to future teaching episodes. When the sharing of feedback becomes a constant part of the administrator–teacher relationship and develops into an accepted, repeated pattern of interaction, then the teacher can begin to expect it and apply it immediately.

What is the best way to deliver this reflective feedback to teachers as directly and immediately as possible? You have several choices. Face-to-face interactions, written notes, e-mailed messages, and checklists beamed via handheld devices are all viable modes of giving feedback. Veteran administrator Kim Marshall (2005) recommends face-to-face feedback as the preferred method whenever possible, since that format allows an exchange of ideas, the opportunity to debate, and the chance to discuss the matter at hand in depth. We respectfully agree in most cases; however, face-to-face feedback is not the top choice for all teachers, nor is it preferable in every situation. In fact, carving out time for effective and uninterrupted face-to-face discussions for four or five teachers per day might be feasible only for Super-Administrators, cape-wearing marvels endowed with superhuman time management skills.

In order to generate truly reflective responses and unbridled critical thought, the administrator must incorporate several variables: the nature of the feedback, the stage of the teacher on the Continuum of Self-Reflection, the intended outcome of the feedback, the confidence of the teacher, the relationships between the teacher and his or her colleagues and between the teacher and his or her instructional coach, and the past history of feedback with this teacher, just to name a few. Several of these factors are described in further detail later in this chapter. For now, we will return to the Hall Walk-Through Reflection Form, our top choice for the medium of frequent feedback.

The administrator uses the reflection form during the 5- to 15-minute walk-through, recording facts and observations to set the scene. The form then becomes a catalyst for action and critical thought when the administrator writes specific feedback in the "Comments" section.

The Nature of the Feedback

Administrator feedback can fall into four major categories: positive comments, general or specific observations, general or specific suggestions, and reflective prompts.

Positive Comments

We all like to receive positive, affirming feedback. Sometimes a pat on the back is just what the doctor ordered. Affirmation can take different forms, including specific praise ("That was a wonderful attempt at asking Maria to respond to Richie's comments") or a simple compliment ("You have a terrific way with children; this classroom has such a positive feel"). In establishing strong relationships, the use of genuine compliments can go a long way.

General or Specific Observations

On many occasions, administrators will conduct a walk-through and note something that causes them to blink twice. Writing that something down can provide an entry point for a later discussion. It can be general ("I have noticed that the quality of student work is improving in your classroom") or specific ("I noted three students drawing pictures during the spelling test") and could even take on the quality of a checklist ("During the read-aloud today, you asked four questions from the evaluation level of Bloom's taxonomy and two from the comprehension level"). Properly made, these observations do not project or imply any evaluative properties. They are meant to report only what was observed, not what the observer thought about it.

General or Specific Suggestions

Depending on the expertise of the teacher, as well as his or her location on the Continuum of Self-Reflection, it may be appropriate for the administrator to provide more direct, specific feedback. These might include affirmations of effective practice ("Do that again next time"), recommendations about ineffective practice ("Next time, do this instead"), or anything in between. These can be used as either positive reinforcement of behaviors we would like to see repeated or corrective advice meant to fix technical errors or misguided decisions so they are not repeated. Frequently, these suggestions ride shotgun with the observations that precede them. For example, after noting that three students were drawing pictures during the spelling test, the administrator could follow with, "You might consider circulating around the room more frequently to help keep students on target." The more specific the suggestion, the more likely the teacher will put it into practice. Generic offerings, such as "Keep working hard to get Jonas to learn to read," won't have the same impact as a more specific suggestion, like "Help Jonas pick out decodable text at his level that he can take home to practice."

Prompts

Most prompt-type feedback comprises what we have come to call "make-you-thinkers," or questions designed to generate some reflective thought on the part of the teacher. These questions don't necessarily require an answer or even a direct response to the administrator; they simply urge the teacher to think critically about instructional decisions, lesson delivery, or whatever it is that prompted the feedback. Often, they replace the suggestion to use a specific strategy and place the onus of thinking, considering, and analyzing onto the shoulders of the teacher. In the example of the three students drawing pictures during the spelling test, the administrator might prompt, "What can you do to help ensure all students are on task?" or even, "Why do you suppose these three students are off task, and what can you do about it?"

A Critical Piece Revealed

Consider carefully the nature of the feedback you give to teachers. You will find that some teachers are hardwired to respond directly to any feedback, whether it's through an impromptu conversation, an e-mail, a heated exchange, a written dissertation, an offhand comment, or a scheduled meeting. Others ruminate on the feedback privately. Still more rely on discussing the feedback with their colleagues to help them discern its meaning and plot a course of action. The intent of delivering feedback is to encourage one or all of these responses—to encourage teachers to reflect on and critically analyze their work in order to improve.

It has been said that people are the result of our collective experiences, but to experiences we would humbly add attitudes, talents, strengths, hopes, dreams, and goals. Every person—every teacher—is as unique as a snowflake, characterized by wildly different strengths and levels of maturity, spiritual harmony, intellectual power, interpersonal charm, comfort with change, and open imagination. Because teachers are unique and special individuals, each responds differently to different types of feedback. Some cannot handle prompts for self-reflection, believing them to contain hidden value-riddled meanings. Others may interpret suggestions as belittling. There are plenty of ways for an administrator to misdeliver feedback to teachers. Effective administrators are careful to tailor their feedback to the recipient so that it can be put to use in a beneficial way.

Pete's Perspective

"Mr. Stennett," a 25-year veteran teacher, asked to have a sit-down with me one morning during summer vacation. Mr. Stennett was a solid teacher, but our relationship during the one year we'd worked together could have been characterized as tentative and standoffish. We had never really bonded or built a strong foundational relationship. But the year had passed without incident.

During the course of our summertime chat, we touched on a number of subjects superficially before Mr. Stennett finally got to the reason behind his request. I could see it took great effort for him to broach the subject, and his eyes welled slightly with tears as he began.

"Pete," he said, avoiding eye contact, "about those walk-through notes you write. . . . I've never felt so professionally insulted in my life." He paused and I grimaced. Putting teachers down or belittling their professionalism is never the intent of the walk-through process, and I was surprised to hear Mr. Stennett say this.

I asked him to give me an example: "What, specifically, have I said that has insulted you?"

Mr. Stennett finally brought his eyes to mine. "You interpret what's going on in my classroom as negative," he said, "and then you ask me to fix it because you think it needs fixing. Well, there's nothing wrong in my classroom, but you want to change everything."

I smiled. "My goal is not to change you or your teaching per se, Mark," I told him. "My goal is to help drive your professional growth and your impact on student learning. Any feedback I've provided through the walk-through process is geared more to make you think about your teaching than anything else." I did not yet ask him why he hadn't come to me sooner, but I did make a mental note to work on this interpersonal relationship with more fervor in the future.

I asked Mr. Stennett if we could go over a few of the walk-through notes I had given him together. He agreed. As we pored over the contents of the notes, I realized two things. First, although Mr. Stennett was a good teacher, his reflective accuracy placed him in the Unaware stage of the Continuum of Self-Reflection. Second, the feedback I had offered him did not meet his needs at all. Self-reflective questioning posed to an Unaware teacher results only in confusion and mystery, and when we're confused we tend to think the worst—which was exactly what happened in this case.

There were three things for me to do. I apologized to Mr. Stennett for any confusion and asked that in the future, he come to me sooner with any questions about my feedback. I also pledged to myself that I would strengthen my relationship with this teacher, in part by scheduling meetings with him on a more regular basis to discuss his professional growth. And finally, I began to link the teacher feedback I delivered more directly to the individual teacher's stage on the Continuum of Self-Reflection.

Cautions

The fact is, some teachers aren't yet ready to accept written feedback at all. A written note left on a teacher's desk after a mini-observation could very well seem intimidating, threatening, or even confrontational if the administrator hasn't established a growth-oriented relationship. Other teachers might be tempted to waltz into the administrator's office to engage in a conversation directly after a formal walk-through. This, too, can be dangerous. When people enter a situation in which they feel uncomfortable or even attacked, a common natural response is to engage in "fight or flight" behavior. A fighting response can spell trouble, leading a teacher to act defensively, justify substandard performance, or provide a pat answer. Abraham Maslow (1962) illuminated this defense, writing, "We tend to be afraid of any knowledge that would . . . make us feel inferior . . . we protect ourselves and our ideal image of ourselves" (p. 173). It is preferable, however, that the teacher sit and ruminate on the feedback for a while; time spent in contemplation might prevent the teacher from dismissing a professional growth opportunity with a defensive justification.

Reflection without feedback, however, is another recipe for disaster. In *Know Yourself? It's a Paradox*, Harris (1981) writes, "In order to know oneself, no amount of introspection or self-examination will suffice. You can analyze yourself for weeks, or meditate for months and you will not get an inch further—any more than you can smell your own breath or laugh when you tickle yourself" (p. 9). Unfortunately, a misfired bit of feedback can inadvertently wedge a monkey wrench into the relationship the administrator so dearly needs to strengthen with each teacher. This is why it becomes so critical to consider each teacher's stage on the Continuum of Self-Reflection prior to providing any sort of feedback. Though human beings are complicated, the goal is simple: Provide the feedback that each individual needs to grow in professional skill and in self-reflective behaviors.

Tailoring Feedback: The Administrator's Roles

When it comes time to deliver feedback to teachers, it is the administrator's responsibility to adapt comments, observations, suggestions, and prompts to fit the needs of each teacher. To help with this aim, we have constructed a version of the Continuum of Self-Reflection that includes specific roles for the administrator (see Figure 12.1). It includes the same goal for teachers at each stage as the one found on the coach's version of the Continuum (see Figure 4.2, pp. 41–42), and provides a series of prompts and stems for offering feedback to teachers in each stage. Ultimately, although the administrator takes a different route with each teacher, it is the shared goal of moving the teacher along the Continuum of Self-Reflection to a point at which the teacher is a reflective, critical thinker that drives this model.

As you know from reading Part II of this book, the behaviors and approaches that characterize teachers in each stage of the continuum precipitate certain coaching strategies. The same holds true for administrative strategies. What follows is a discussion about the commonalities found in teachers in each stage, your role as the administrator in supporting each teacher's growth, and a detailed look at the feedback prompts that will most likely result in increased effectiveness and self-reflection from individual teachers. Remember, none of these approaches will have any significant effect without a positive, mutually respectful, growth-oriented relationship between the administrator and each individual teacher. We'll say it a hundred times, because it's that important: Education is a people business, and relationships are key.

Director: Working with Teachers in the Unaware Stage

You will recall that teachers in the Unaware stage of the Continuum have little or no awareness of best practices in instruction, often prefer scripted lessons, and are commonly in survival mode, just trying to get through the day. It could even be that an Unaware teacher believes he or she is using effective instruction, but in reality, it's all about going through the motions. The common goal shared by the coach and administrator when working with these teachers is *to create awareness of the need for change and foster a desire to learn.*

Whereas the coach's role in working with an Unaware teacher is to become an unconditional partner, the administrator takes a different, more directive tack in order to increase the frequency with which the teacher engages in sound instructional practices. In a sense, you need to approach an Unaware teacher thinking, "If I can change this teacher's behavior, I can then work on the teacher's beliefs." Ideally, the teacher will then engage in new learning ("what to do") and begin to grasp the rationale ("why to do it"), prompting future learning and action.

Feedback in the Director Role

To accomplish this task, the administrator should provide very specific, detailed feedback to the teacher. To reinforce strategies that worked and ought to

Figure 12.1

The Continuum of Self-Reflection: Administrator's Model

Teacher's Reflective Tendencies	Related Classroom Characteristics	Your Role as Administrator	Sample Feedback Prompts to Encourage Reflective Growth
• Demonstrates little or no awareness of instructional reality in the classroom • Focuses on routine • Exhibits the best of intentions • Expresses confusion about own role in learning • Collaborates with colleagues on a superficial level • Defines problems inaccurately • Focuses on the job itself—the act of teaching	• Scripted lessons, with little or no teacher modeling • Passive learning, with little or no student interaction • Lessons built on direct instruction and assignments • Little or no evidence of systematic, standards-based planning • No differentiation of instruction • Little or no awareness of effective time management • No link between instruction and assessment • Little effort to make curriculum relevant to students	*Director* • Encourage repeated future use of an effective instructional approach • Compliment an attempted use of an effective instructional strategy (with a specific suggestion for improvement) • Discourage future use of an ineffective instructional approach	• I noticed you used _____, and it was effective; use it whenever you want your students to _____. • Terrific job attempting longer wait time; next time, count to five in your head before calling on a student. • I observed four students engaged in side-talk; try asking them to turn to their partner to regain their focus. • You have a real talent for complimenting students; use that to praise their ideas, not just their penmanship. • In this lesson, you were suggesting great reading strategies; however, few students stopped working to listen. Try insisting that all students drop everything when you ring a chime in the room. • Judging by the look on your face, that transition did not go as smoothly as you planned; come see me when you get a minute and we'll talk about some strategies to use.

Unaware Stage

Capacity-Building Goal: *To create awareness of the need for change and foster a desire to learn*

Teacher's Reflective Tendencies	Related Classroom Characteristics	Your Role as Administrator	Sample Feedback Prompts to Encourage Reflective Growth
• Demonstrates a consistent "knowing–doing" gap • Can ambiguously cite research to support current teaching methods • Makes excuses for problems • Demonstrates limited ability to evaluate problems • Becomes easily distracted from goals • Collaborates inconsistently with colleagues • Disregards others' ideas • Focuses first on self	• Instruction designed for teacher convenience • Short-term planning evident, yet inconsistent • Occasional links between instruction and assessment • Little student engagement in active, meaningful learning • Little problem solving from students • Occasional differentiation of instruction • Noticeable swings in instructional approaches	*Navigator* • Establish a focus for goal setting • Encourage consistency in application of effective instructional practices • Redirect teaching behaviors toward the proper heading • Extend self-reflective efforts	• I noticed you used _____, and it was effective. Why do you think it worked so well? • Let's talk about goal setting. Classroom management seems to be an area that you're working on; perhaps that is a good place to start our conversation. • I see you're attempting _____. What support can I provide to help you keep that focus? • Yesterday I observed your students working cooperatively; today, they are working independently. How did you determine the lesson structure for these classes? • This was a fun lesson to observe. Did the students understand the learning objective? How do you know? • Your interaction with students was very positive and encouraging today. Keep it up! You'll see the gains! • Three students seemed perplexed by your questioning. Why do you think that happened? What can you do?

Conscious Stage

Capacity-Building Goal: *To motivate and show how to apply pedagogical knowledge consistently*

Figure 12.1—*(continued)*

The Continuum of Self-Reflection: Administrator's Model

	Teacher's Reflective Tendencies	Related Classroom Characteristics	Your Role as Administrator	Sample Feedback Prompts to Encourage Reflective Growth
Action Stage	• Accepts responsibility for the success of all students and for own personal growth • Evaluates issues and situations objectively • Seeks to incorporate research-based concepts and strategies • Reflects upon teaching only after the action • Believes in only one "right" way of doing things • Struggles to identify solutions to long-term problems • Receives feedback well, then enters a critical loop • Collaborates on a limited basis with colleagues • Focuses on the *science* of teaching	• Regular use of assessment to monitor student progress • Consistent application of best-practice instructional strategies • Lessons linked to standards • Evidence of limited long-term planning • Classroom appears functional, but gaps are lurking	*Prompter* • Encourage reflection to support effective instructional choices • Question the impact of certain instructional strategies • Consider alternative approaches or points of view • Propose continued professional learning	• I noticed you used _____. Was it effective? How do you know? • Terrific job asking higher-order thinking questions. Did that contribute to a deeper understanding of the material? How can you tell? What does this tell you about your questioning strategies? • When and how do you decide which questions to ask students? • What are some strategies you can use to engage some of your reluctant writers? • I know you gave a pre-assessment before this math unit. How closely is this lesson related to the results of that formative assessment? • Today your students were busy with a lot of worksheet tasks. You have told me you believe in paper-and-pencil activities. How can you better blend that goal with the students' goal of meeting learning targets? • You told your students not to talk during the review activity. What would happen if you allowed them to investigate their answers together? Would they be any less prepared for the final test?

Capacity-Building Goal: *To build on experience and help strengthen expertise*

Teacher's Reflective Tendencies	Related Classroom Characteristics	Your Role as Administrator	Sample Feedback Prompts to Encourage Reflective Growth
Refinement Stage • Reflects before, during, and after taking action • Recognizes that there are multiple "right" courses of action • Maintains a vast repertoire of instructional strategies • Engages in action research as common practice • Modifies lessons and plans to meet students' needs • Pursues opportunities to work and learn with colleagues • Thinks beyond the classroom • Focuses on the *art* of teaching	• Assessment drives daily instruction • Students largely responsible for their own learning • Multiple instructional strategies in use	*Challenger* • Drive personal reflection • Introduce new ideas • Serve as devil's advocate • Encourage involvement in leadership	• In today's lesson you asked terrific follow-up questions. Are these planned in advance or off the cuff? • I read a great article in *Educational Leadership* about this. I'll put a copy in your mailbox—let me know what you think about it. • During this lesson, your teaching engaged students in a variety of formats; however, there were still two students that appeared disengaged throughout. What is your explanation, and what can you do differently to reel them in? • I'm not sure I understand the way you've grouped students for this assignment. Can you explain your thinking to me? • I observed virtually the same lesson yesterday in _____'s classroom, and she did it a different way. This might be a good idea to participate in a lesson study to compare methods and results. Would you like me to facilitate that discussion? • This was a good example of bringing the lesson to life. Would you be willing to share it (and its results) with your grade-level colleagues?

Capacity-Building Goal: *To encourage long-term growth and continued reflection*

be repeated, give very specific praise, complimenting the teacher on good use of a solid instructional practice. To deter strategies that did not work and ought to be eliminated, provide specific instructions for what to do differently next time. This is not a time to waffle back and forth with ambiguous feedback; rather, it is a time for clarity, specificity, and transparent expectations.

To help clarify how you might use the feedback prompts and stems included in the administrator's model of the Continuum of Self-Reflection (see Figure 12.1) in the application of this approach, let's look at a few examples, guided by the primary purpose of the feedback.

Specific praise to encourage repeated future use of an effective instructional approach. If the teacher engages in a behavior that works (and this practice isn't usually implemented), the administrator should praise the effort. For example, if the teacher asks students to spell the word *dog* with their fingers in the sky while the teacher writes it on the board (thus keeping the majority of the students actively engaged in the lesson), appropriate feedback might be something like this: "I noticed you asked your students to skywrite, and it worked beautifully; do that whenever you need to keep the students actively engaged."

Specific praise to compliment an attempted use of an effective instructional strategy (with a specific suggestion for improvement). If the teacher attempts an effective strategy that does not go exactly as planned, the administrator should praise the attempt but be equally clear about the modification. For example, if the teacher tries to ask a higher-order thinking question during a read-aloud with students but the question comes out unclear, you could say, "Great attempt at incorporating higher-order questioning to help your students think more deeply about the text, though I noticed you stumbled on the delivery. Next time, prepare your questions in advance and write them on a sticky note in the book."

Specific corrective feedback to discourage future use of an ineffective instructional approach. If the teacher uses a faulty strategy, the administrator should provide specific feedback with clear expectations for future alternative actions. For example, if the teacher talks over students' voices while trying to give directions, you could say, "While the students were working and chatting, you attempted to give further directions and needed to raise your voice. Many of the students continued to work and chat throughout the directions. Try this next time: Insist that every single student 'gives you five,' then proceed with your directions. It won't help them if they can't hear it!"

Navigator: Working with Teachers in the Conscious Stage

Teachers in the Conscious stage provide ample real-life illustrations of the infamous "knowing–doing gap" (Pfeffer & Sutton, 2000). Often, a Conscious teacher can recite the rationale for specific practices but does not apply them in the classroom. This disconnect occurs for a variety of reasons. The teacher may not believe it will work with this class, may be a bit overwhelmed and distracted, or may possibly lack adequate motivation. Regardless of the causes, Conscious teachers are inconsistent in "walking the talk" and need frequent feedback (daily, whenever possible). The common goal shared by the administrator and coach when working with these teachers is *to motivate them and show them how to apply pedagogical knowledge more consistently.*

In working with teachers in the Conscious stage, the coach and administrator engage in very similar roles. Both emphasize short-term goal setting, establishing a clear vision, and providing frequent feedback. However, whereas the coach sets a collaborative goal with a Conscious teacher and provides support as a motivator and strategist, your role is to focus on keeping the teacher's attention on the agreed-upon course—in other words, acting as a navigator.

Feedback in the Navigator Role

To accomplish this task, the administrator provides detailed, specific feedback, with positive praise as appropriate, with great frequency. Because of their lack of consistency, Conscious-stage teachers benefit from almost daily support and feedback. Couple this observational feedback with a direct question, often one for which both you and teacher have an agreed-upon answer. In a sense, you ask leading questions, intending to usher the teacher along the path the two of you have established together. This strategy works because the teacher already knows some of the elements of best practices; the responsibility to hold the teacher accountable for doing what he or she knows to do now rests on your administrative shoulders. Goal setting follows the same protocol: Your role is to engage the teacher in a directive/collaborative approach, which means meeting together but steering the conversation to a predetermined outcome.

Specific feedback to establish a focus for goal setting. If the teacher demonstrates an area of focus (a weakness, the lack of a particular skill, or another element of teaching that could use some strengthening), you can guide the goal-setting conversation to that end. For example, if the teacher is struggling with some behavioral issues in class, pursue this rather than getting distracted by guided-reading strategies or another less dire area: "Classroom management seems to be an area you are working on; perhaps that is a good place to start our conversation. Come see me and we'll chat about it."

Specific feedback to encourage consistent application of effective instructional practices. A teacher who delivers good teaching sometimes but not all the time needs daily, specific feedback. Encourage the teacher to repeat that good teaching strategy all the time with feedback like this: "I noticed you required Jessica to defend her answer during the class discussion. Wonderful! How does that strategy deepen Jessica's understanding of the content?"

Specific feedback to redirect teaching behaviors toward the proper heading. If the teacher begins to stray from the stated goal, you can help by calibrating the teacher's instructional compass. For example, if the teacher and you have set a goal for the teacher to increase the use of cooperative learning strategies in the classroom, but you observe a lecture and independent work format during a walk-through, you might say, "One of your individual goals is to increase cooperative learning activities; today I observed 15 minutes of lecture and independent work. What opportunities could you have used to increase the time and manner that students work together?"

Specific feedback to extend self-reflective efforts. The teacher who demonstrates effective teaching strategies on a consistent basis may be ripe to wrestle with more open-ended questioning. For example, if the teacher repeatedly displays and discusses the lesson's learning targets with the class (an area of focus for this teacher), you could ask the teacher to spread his or her intellectual wings a bit with this feedback: "You've done a nice job sharing the learning objective with your class. Did the students understand the learning objective? How do you know?"

Prompter: Working with Teachers in the Action Stage

Teachers in the Action stage are motivated to make productive changes to their teaching performance. An Action teacher is open to constructive feedback, attempts to act on new information, and seeks out the "correct" solution to instructional "problems." This tendency sometimes provides a narrow scope of new learning, and he or she may have difficulty identifying solutions to long-term problems. The common goal that administrator and coach share when working with these teachers is *to build on experience and help strengthen expertise.*

In Chapter 7 we described the coach's role in the Action stage as that of a mentor. The administrator's concurrent role is to provide regular feedback and encouragement, while capitalizing on the Action teacher's openness and inquisitiveness by providing a relentless array of reflective questions. In this manner, the administrator serves as a prompter, generating the teacher's reflective thought.

Feedback in the Prompter Role

To accomplish this task, the administrator should provide specific feedback, with specific positive praise as appropriate, on a regular basis. Since Action-stage teachers are open to new learning and are willing to implement new strategies in their classrooms, complement this frequent feedback by persistently asking open-ended questions to extend the teachers' thinking. In this way, Action teachers will consider the rationale behind their decisions, investigate divergent points of view, attempt alternative courses of action to solve problems, and meditate on the effectiveness of their choices. Such questioning will invariably send Action teachers to their instructional coach or colleagues for further discussion. This yields two positive additional benefits: the coach (as a bona fide expert) shares expertise to help clarify the teachers' questions, and the teachers together invest some time in intense collaborative problem solving. Both, in turn, generate further reflective thought and investigative analysis, which lead to additional collaboration. The following are some examples of administrator feedback that can start the wheel turning.

Specific feedback to encourage reflection in support of effective instructional choices. If the teacher makes effective teaching decisions, pose a reflective question to engage the teacher in a critical assessment of the instructional practice. Force the issue of self-reflective practice. For example, if the teacher asks questions from several levels of Bloom's taxonomy during a math investigation, you could support that with feedback like this: "Nice job of varying your questioning to hit all depths. Did that contribute to the students' deeper understanding of the material? How can you tell? What does this tell you about your questioning strategies?"

Specific feedback to question the impact of certain instructional strategies. If the teacher makes teaching decisions that may or may not have positive (or lasting) effects, a reflective question could help determine the future use of that strategy. For example, if the teacher implements a new system in which a chime is rung two times to gather students' attention prior to giving new directions, you could respond, "I noticed you've begun a transition-streamlining strategy. Is it effective? What evidence do you have to support that?"

Specific feedback to consider alternative approaches or points of view. If the teacher seems drawn to a specific strategy that usually returns positive result, but that strategy is not proving effective in certain situations, it may be time to help the teacher mull over new methods. This is critical to helping the teacher see beyond the one "right" way of teaching a lesson or a particular concept. For example, if the teacher uses zany prompts to inspire students to write creatively in their journals but a handful of students remain reluctant to write, you could make a suggestion like this: "Your prompts are intriguing and captivate the majority of the students in your class. Are all the students engaged in creative writing as a result? Is there another approach you might take to tap into those hesitant writers' creativity?"

Specific feedback to propose continued professional learning. If the teacher seems to be handling the day-to-day challenges of teaching and appears ready to engulf the "next steps" of professional development, the administrator can support the process by suggesting a new element of individual growth. You could say, for example, "I see a lot of good things in your classroom. Is there an area on which you'd like to focus some additional energy? We have some staff development funds that might cover some professional reading or the registration for a seminar. I'd be glad to talk to you about the possibilities—come see me when you get a chance."

Challenger: Working with Teachers in the Refinement Stage

Teachers in the Refinement stage generally have considerable knowledge and experience using best practices in their classrooms. Refinement teachers are responsive to the needs and interests of individual learners in the classroom, often adapting teaching strategies and lesson components on the fly to support learners. They are constantly yearning to learn more, enraptured with the notion of self-improvement, and perfect examples of the overused term "lifelong learner." They plan, set goals, and establish high expectations for themselves, their students, their colleagues, and everyone around them. True collaborators, Refinement-stage teachers seek out their colleagues to engage in rich, professional conversations that challenge their thinking. Refinement teachers' engines are always humming. When working with these teachers, the administrator's and coach's common goal is *to encourage long-term growth and continued reflection.*

With teachers in the Refinement stage, the coach and administrator take very similar actions. The coach, no longer needed to impart knowledge as a teaching expert per se, serves more as a sounding board and partner in deep pedagogical and philosophical investigations. The administrator, similarly, serves to challenge the teachers' thinking, making them reflect often, engage in and lead professional discussions, and clarify their thought processes.

Feedback in the Challenger Role

To accomplish this task, the administrator should provide specific feedback, with specific positive praise as appropriate, and pose deep, challenging reflective questions to test Refinement teachers' beliefs, perceptions, biases, knowledge, creativity, and professional practice. After establishing a respectful, results-driven, growth-oriented professional relationship with the teacher, begin the interrogation. Because Refinement teachers are predisposed to critical thought, they need tough probes and questions that force them out of their comfort zone to consider new paths, extend their thinking, examine their beliefs and values, and debate their positions. These actions will shuttle Refinement teachers into deep, reflective dialogue with themselves and their colleagues, as well as send them to seek guidance from extensive professional resources. Because they often have tremendous amounts of experience, knowledge, skill, and wherewithal, they might consider it an obligation to share these in a collaborative format through leadership roles, professional development sessions, or mentoring programs.

Although providing feedback that a Refinement teacher can use may seem like a daunting challenge, here are some examples that can help start the crucial conversations.

Specific feedback to drive personal reflection. If the teacher uses a variety of instructional strategies with success, the administrator may want to determine if the teacher is cognizant of these selections. Such reflective feedback may look like this: "In today's lesson, you asked terrific follow-up questions; how do you filter the information to develop these questions? Do you plan them in advance? How do you know when enough is enough for one student's question and it's time to move along?"

Specific feedback to introduce new ideas. If the teacher is routinely producing high-quality lessons with a solid repertoire of teaching skills and demonstrates a desire to learn more (or to learn about something different), the administrator can facilitate this growth. Your feedback could take this direction: "I was noticing the different ways you engaged students in the learning during this lesson. There is an interesting article on brain research and learning styles in this month's *Educational Leadership*. I'll put a copy in your mailbox, and then we can talk about it."

Specific feedback to serve as devil's advocate. If the teacher makes an instructional decision that may or may not produce perfect results, the administrator can help confirm the teacher's thinking, dismantle the thinking, or provide the arena for the thinking to venture to parts unknown, depending on the depth and quality of the reflection. Your feedback might go something like this: "I know you've grouped your students intentionally by ability level for this assignment; however, it's quite possible that this project calls for heterogeneous groups. Can you explain your rationale to me?"

Specific feedback to encourage involvement in leadership. A teacher who excels in a certain area of teaching (it will likely be difficult to narrow it down to one!) can extend his or her professional wings and lift the group to a higher level by sharing this practice with grade-level or subject-area teams, the entire staff, or another compilation of professionals. You might say, "This strategy of mind-mapping was a terrific example of bringing the lesson to life. Would you be willing to share it (and its results) with all the primary grade teachers at next week's staff meeting?"

In Figure 12.2, you'll find a summary of the types of feedback suitable for teachers in each stage of the Continuum of Self-Reflection.

Figure 12.2	
Types of Feedback by Continuum Stage	
Continuum Stage	**Feedback Type**
Unaware	Positive praise and specific suggestions
Conscious	Specific observations and leading prompts
Action	Specific observations and open prompts
Refinement	Specific observations and challenging prompts

It Bears Repeating

Honest, constructive, reflective feedback is an essential building block of a strong administrator–teacher relationship. If the relationship is strong between administrator and teacher, the likelihood of professional growth and enhanced skill increases. The trust between the teacher and the administrator increases. The depth and honesty with which they can engage in growth-oriented discussions increase. With a strong relationship, we can overturn the conventional wisdom that openness and evaluation are incompatible on its ear and move on to discuss another unexpected harmonious pairing: teacher evaluation and professional development.

13

Development and Evaluation

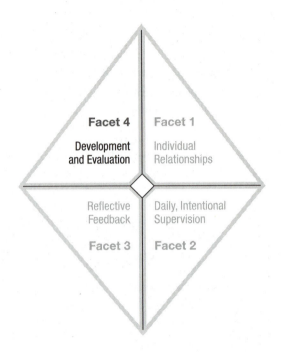

Facet 4
Development and Evaluation

Facet 1
Individual Relationships

Reflective Feedback

Daily, Intentional Supervision

Facet 3

Facet 2

You know your teachers. You have identified where they are on the Continuum of Self-Reflection. You have established team goals for all and individual goals for many. You've begun to engage in walk-throughs to provide teachers with specific, reflective feedback. What's next? How do you go on to work with each teacher? How do you approach the work with each team? What specific steps can you take to help bring about Strength-Based School Improvement—a process that encompasses helping all teachers expand their knowledge, augment their instructional strategies, improve their efficiency, and, perhaps most pointedly, increase their self-reflective abilities and behaviors? It's a tall order.

The DVD of the movie *Miracle* (2005), a dramatization of the 1980 U.S. Olympic hockey team's improbable gold medal win, includes a great conversation between Coach Herb Brooks and Kurt Russell, the actor who played Coach Brooks in the film. Brooks insists that his responsibility to his players was to "pull the greatness out of them." He was a tough cookie on the outside, demanding perfection and superiority at every turn, but he also identified the unique and special talents—the strengths—that each player possessed and derived a plan to help draw each individual's excellence to the forefront. So it is, or so it *should be*, with school administrators and teachers.

Engaging in the intentional, feedback-rich Hall Walk-Through process is a start. Encouraging teachers to participate in deep, reflective inquiry and professional dialogue keeps the momentum going. Eventually, however, two realities set in for the school administrator. First, all teachers hit a point beyond which their experience and knowledge are limited and individualized professional development is necessary to continue their growth. And second, because the administrator is also the teachers' evaluator, the administrator is obligated to follow the policies in place that dictate an accurate annual performance review. Facet 4 of the Administrator's Responsibilities Diamond addresses both embedded professional development and teacher evaluation.

Teacher Evaluations and the Status Quo

Let's start by turning our attention to teacher evaluation, one of the administrator's most critical responsibilities. In every district we've ever visited or researched, there is a stringent set of regulations governing the what, how, when, and where of teacher evaluation. The *why* of it, however, frequently gets lost in the avalanche of paperwork, scheduled observations, formal meetings, and sterile write-ups. We seem to be forgetting what the entire process is for.

Pete's Perspective

Examining the case of "Mrs. Walstad," a teacher I met during my first year as a building administrator, is one way to help make sense of the teacher evaluation process. At the time, my experiences as a teacher and my training as an administrator supported my belief that the clinical supervision model—more aptly described as a clinical *evaluation* model—was the way to go when assessing teacher performance.

Mrs. Walstad was a 6th grade teacher. She taught the equivalent of six classes per day (two reading and one each of math, science, social studies, and language arts) for 180 school days—that's 1,080 class periods in a single school year, a healthy working assignment. Using the clinical evaluation process, Mrs. Walstad and I sat down together early in the year to schedule the three required classroom observations.

Prior to each of these observation periods, Mrs. Walstad and I discussed what I would see, what the intended learning targets were, and some elements of lesson construction and planning. Then I plunked myself down in the middle of her classroom, taking copious notes and thoroughly digesting the goings-on. After each observation, we sat down again, resuming our conversation about the lesson outcomes. Mrs. Walstad received plenty of feedback on her lessons. She and I occasionally even pored over student data to correlate the teaching with the learning. I was quite sure that I knew everything I needed to know about this teacher.

Then, based on the three classroom observations and the teaching element discussions, I proceeded to write Mrs. Walstad's annual teacher evaluation document. Despite having observed less than 1 percent of her teaching during the school year (3 lessons out of 1,080), I happily checked off the requisite boxes and cheerfully wrote the compulsory narrative. Mrs. Walstad was free to go, and I moved on to the next teacher, continuing, zombie-like, through the steps of clinical evaluation.

Was Mrs. Walstad a better teacher for having gone through that process? I wanted to believe so, but I wasn't sure. Did my reams of notes and deluge of feedback contribute to greater student success in her classroom? I did not have the data to make such correlations. Was the written evaluation document an accurate reflection of the work Mrs. Walstad did over the entire school year? I knew that the answer to that, sadly, was an emphatic *no*. Over 99 percent of her teaching had gone unobserved. But the question that gnawed on me most was this: Was any of my work differentiated for the strengths and needs of Mrs. Walstad as a teacher and as a person?

Then a thought struck me, and I wrote it down: "To you, Mrs. Walstad is one of 32 teachers you'll be evaluating this year. To Mrs. Walstad, she is one of one. Treat her that way."

The Missing Link(s)

We have a radical idea to propose. In order to make the teacher evaluation process beneficial to everyone involved, let's coordinate the teacher's formal assessment with three vital elements:

1. The teacher's individual and team goals
2. The teacher's professional development plan
3. The teacher's actual performance throughout the school year

Because the teacher's progress toward meeting individual and team goals requires the analysis of student data, an element of "level two effectiveness" (as introduced in Chapter 1) becomes an important part of the evaluation. As the teacher's professional development plan is directly related to skills, strategies, and knowledge, these components are likewise included. And in the final analysis, most teacher evaluation systems agree that an intended goal is to provide the teacher with an annual performance review—so why not make it just that?

Kim Marshall (2005), a longtime school administrator in Boston, discusses 10 flaws in the current teacher evaluation process in his article "It's Time to Rethink Teacher Supervision and Evaluation." At the top of the list is that we "evaluate only a tiny amount of teaching" (p. 728). How many of us fulfill only the minimum requirements of classroom observations, spending one or two long lessons recording the teacher's actions to include in that teacher's performance evaluation? What are the odds that we're observing a dog-and-pony show? In such a high-stakes event, what confidence can we have that the teacher is performing as he or she normally performs and that these two lessons are representative of every lesson in that classroom?

This brings us back to the *why* of teacher evaluation. Charlotte Danielson and Thomas McGreal (2000) made it very clear in their breakthrough book, *Teacher Evaluation to Enhance Professional Practice*, that the "two principal functions of teacher evaluation are (1) quality assurance, and (2) professional development" (p. 8). Teacher evaluation, then, is both summative and formative. Demonstrating accountability means that we need to show that all the teachers currently employed in our schools measure up to a certain professional standard—that's the summative piece. But we have an obligation to help our teachers grow and improve their professional practice—the formative element.

Danielson and McGreal's model is one that we embrace fully. It involves three "tracks," or evaluation structures, into which the teachers fall: Track I, for beginning or nontenured teachers; Track II, for competent, tenured staff (the majority of teachers in the building); and Track III, for teachers about whom you have performance concerns or who are not demonstrating minimum competency standards.

No matter which track each teacher falls into, the entire evaluation process must be authentic—that is, the administrator must observe actual teaching and learning "in the wild." Frequent unannounced mini-observations, using the Hall Walk-Through process, provide the ideal vehicle to accomplish this goal. Through walk-throughs and rounds, the administrator can accrue a massive amount of data regarding *actual* teaching and learning and can observe the teacher and students in their natural environment.

For those teachers in Track I (beginning teachers for whom the evaluation document could make the difference between renewal and nonrenewal of a contract) and Track III (teachers with performance concerns that may affect the quality of education in the school), the administrator may still need to undergo the clinical evaluation process. But the steps of the Hall Walk-Through allow the administrator to collect adequate data, in a way approved by any negotiated agreement, that indicate whether or not the teacher is capable of meeting the minimum expectation of teaching performance. Lest we gave the impression earlier that the clinical evaluation process had no place in education, we would like to be clear: It may not work effectively for all teachers in all situations, but it is essential to some teachers in some circumstances.

For the great majority of the other teachers in the school—those with no performance concerns—walk-throughs and rounds can be a more than sufficient exercise in authentic teacher observation, allowing the administrator to focus on professional development with these teachers.

Develop a Plan of Attack

As you strive to maximize the strengths and potential of every individual teacher on staff, you necessarily need to find and fortify the links among performance, potential, and evaluation. Let's begin by addressing the element of individualized professional growth. To assist with the planning of this professional development approach, it is appropriate to review each teacher's individual goals and each team's common goal. If the school has an instructional coach or a mentor, this would be the time to meet with that person to review those goals to get the necessary supports in place for each individual teacher. Remember that the administrator's role is to coordinate professional development plans and to monitor growth, not necessarily to provide the professional development directly.

What follows is a collection of effective professional development approaches. They all have their strengths and weaknesses, and they may not all work for every teacher. The savvy administrator must select wisely depending on the goal, the individual in question, the teacher's stage on the Continuum of Self-Reflection, and other factors. Each of the professional development endeavors covered here is accompanied by a reference for further information and support.

Lesson study. The teacher selects an appropriate standard, assesses the students' understanding, creates a plan to teach it effectively, and measures the results. This is a powerful activity when done in a team setting. (See Schmoker, 2006.)

Collegial observations. The teacher spends a half-day observing colleagues within the building, either at the same grade level or in a common subject, and discusses observations afterward, with either a coach or the teachers observed. (See DuFour & Eaker, 1998.)

Peer coaching. A pair of teachers alternate periods observing each other and collecting data to share. Focusing on a particular aspect of instruction, the pair then exchanges information. (See Glatthorn, 1997.)

Workshop/outside expert consultation. Sometimes, we just need to hear good information from a reputable source, even if it's the same information we've heard time and again locally. In addition, workshops can be tremendously motivating and informative for some. (See Allington & Cunningham, 2007.)

Visitation. A visit to a neighboring school with similar characteristics, especially if it has experienced success in the arena in which your goal is set, can yield significant dividends. Here we can see great ideas in action, and they're not too far away. (See Hall, 2004.)

Action research. This is the gist of the "professional development approach," really. Like a lesson study for an entire unit, an action research plan isolates instructional focus points and returns information about their effectiveness. (See Sagor, 1991.)

Modeled/demonstration lessons. Coaches are particularly useful when it comes to modeling lessons in a specific teacher's classroom. This gives teachers an opportunity to see best practice in action with their own students, and they can draw comparisons between theory and implementation more readily. (See Moran, 2007.)

Portfolio development. As a teacher attempts new strategies, implements new learning, and collects data, he or she can maintain a professional portfolio detailing these steps and the results, thus providing the evidentiary artifacts that support continued learning. (See Danielson & McGreal, 2000.)

Diagnostic observation. The coach observes the teacher for multiple class periods, seeking trends, strengths, and/or areas of need. In a debriefing session, the coach and teacher discuss particular strategies to apply immediately. (See Glatthorn, 1997.)

Book study. This powerful group learning tool includes time spent with a common professional text. Reading a book on guided reading, for instance, and then coming together to discuss the ideas presented and practical ways to apply the new learning offers many viewpoints on a common subject. (See Allington & Cunningham, 2007.)

Literature review. Often, teachers select an intervention strategy based upon what amounts to hearsay. Rather than shoot from the hip, these teachers could conduct their own research, review the findings, and discuss them or present a short summary to the staff explaining an instructional method they wish to try. (See Danielson & McGreal, 2000.)

Reflective journaling. One of the primary tenets of our strength-based approach is to encourage teacher reflection; providing a journal (and time to fill it up) can nudge teachers toward a more self-reflective approach to their daily duties. (See Brookfield, 1995.)

Official collaborative time. If it is possible through districtwide scheduling (on early-release or delayed-start days) or schoolwide planning (common prep times for teachers with like assignments), a meeting time on a regular basis can help to ensure that all team members are on the same page and are communicating with one another. (See DuFour & Eaker, 1998.)

Each of these approaches is intended to drive individual teachers' professional growth through increasing knowledge, direct reflective inquiry, or additional experiential feedback. Though geared for the Track II teachers (those who are already on track), the idea of professional development should be investigated with due diligence for every teacher. Keep in mind that because not every teacher is ready and willing to tackle new tasks related to professional development, the relationships among teacher, coach, and administrator are critical. When the time to pursue these opportunities and the individuals are in alignment, however, they can offer a plethora of choices to foster growth.

Coupling the frequent monitoring of teaching and learning that occurs during rounds with the regular feedback cycle of the Hall Walk-Through and then adding a healthy dose of an intentional professional development plan will help the great majority of teachers move forward in their growth. The tools have been laid out and are now at our disposal; it's time to put them to work.

Concluding Thoughts

The idea of improving our schools is not new. The intent to increase teachers' skills has been bandied about for generations. Coupling the two, then, with intentional work by administrators and coaches to develop each individual teacher's strengths, abilities, and potential only makes sense. Though the work may seem daunting, it is quite doable. As you've read, it's a matter of building and maintaining strong relationships with every single teacher on staff. It's a matter of encouraging self-reflection through individualized coaching and providing specific, targeted administrative feedback. It's a matter of taking what we've learned and putting it to practical use. Using this model of coaching for reflective growth, offering immediate supervisory feedback, and monitoring teachers' progress along the Continuum of Self-Reflection are at the heart of the Strength-Based School Improvement mission. When we engage in a strength-based approach, it becomes possible to close every gap known to education, especially the vast and mysteriously prevalent knowing–doing gap.

The Essential Partnership

One theme that we have woven throughout this book is the importance of the partnership between the administrator and the coach. Within the context of any single school, interpersonal dynamics can be intense and politics can be staggering. Both coach and administrator must take careful measures to ensure that positive working relationships among all parties remain intact, and one of the most effective ways for them to do that is to coordinate their work as allies and approach their responsibilities in concert. You may still have some questions about how to put this theory into practice. Let our answers to the following questions guide you as you approach this challenge.

When and how should the administrator and coach sit down together? The short answer is this: whenever possible. We know the realities of the demands of both jobs leave us gasping for air on a *normal* day; however, we also know the benefits of maintaining an open avenue of communication between the two. It's tremendously valuable for administrator and coach to sit down to talk and learn about each other, to communicate expectations, to discuss philosophy, to share the vision, and to specify the details of their work. The more that each can demonstrate that they are both on the same page, the more effective their work with teachers will be. Coordination and communication are critical components to an effective coaching/administrating plan. We recommend scheduling a time, perhaps weekly or biweekly, that both parties can commit to attending regularly.

How do both parties establish a trusting relationship? Our advice is simple: Start by being professional. Trust can be a dicey political element—easy to lose and nearly impossible to rebuild—and both coach and administrator should approach their relationship with honesty, openness, transparency, and follow-through. Just as members of a professional learning community sit down to establish their group's norms prior to engaging in tough work (DuFour & Eaker, 1998), so should members of the administrator–coach dyad. Agreeing upon boundaries, expectations, responsibilities, and standards will help ease the strain when difficult conversations arise, as they always will. And, whenever in doubt, respond to conflict, gossip, emotions, and events like a professional; this approach may help keep the moral compass calibrated.

To what extent should coaches and administrators discuss individual teachers? This is perhaps the most controversial question on the list. Like the well-publicized doctor–patient privilege, there exists a de facto administrator–teacher privilege that limits the degree to which an administrator can discuss the professional work of a teacher with a fellow teacher. However, in order for the coach and administrator to approach their work with individual teachers, it's essential that they discuss the teachers together. This elevates the issue to one of trust on all three sides of the relationship-triangulation triad.

The best way to avoid misspeaking about any individual teacher is to keep the conversation focused on that teacher's stage on the Continuum of Self-Reflection. Through careful discussion of reflective tendencies and classroom characteristics, the coach and administrator can arrive at a consensus about where each teacher is on the Continuum. It's important, especially for the coach's sake, to keep the role division between administrator and coach separate when necessary. An unscrupulous administrator could invite the coach to participate in a discussion of a teacher's performance, which might lead to a rather unfortunate, evaluative conversation—and that's no place for a coach to be, ever. (Refer to Figure 2.2, on page 22 for the delineation of coach and administrator roles.)

These discussions help the coach to understand the administrator's approach to teachers in certain stages on the Continuum and the administrator to be aware of the coach's approach. Each knows what the other is doing to help develop that teacher's skills and reflective behaviors. If we approach our work from those two angles (and if we set up our teachers in appropriate teams with worthwhile goals), we can make heady gains toward building all teachers' capacity.

Examples from the Field

In order to best illustrate this process, especially the extent to which the administrator and coach must coordinate their work with one another, we thought it appropriate to extend the stories of the teachers discussed in the "Alisa's Approaches" sections of the book and share the approaches taken by both coach (Alisa) and administrator (Pete) when they worked with these teachers. Each teacher falls within a different stage of the Continuum of Self-Reflection. As you read their stories, we invite you to refer back to the coach's version of the Continuum to analyze Alisa's strategies, and check with the administrator's version of the Continuum to understand Pete's actions. The figure on pages 172–173 shows a side-by-side look at the coach's and administrator's roles with teachers in each stage of the Continuum of Self-Reflection.

The Continuum of Self-Reflection: Dual Model

DOWNLOAD

	Teacher's Reflective Tendencies	Related Classroom Characteristics	The Coach's Role	The Administrator's Role
Unaware Stage	• Demonstrates little or no awareness of instructional reality in the classroom • Focuses on routine • Exhibits the best of intentions • Expresses confusion about own role in learning • Collaborates with colleagues on a superficial level • Defines problems inaccurately • Focuses on the job itself—the act of teaching	• Scripted lessons, with little or no teacher modeling • Passive learning, with little or no student interaction • Lessons built on direct instruction and assignments. • Little or no evidence of systematic, standards-based planning • No differentiation of instruction • Little or no awareness of effective time management • No link between instruction and assessment • Little effort to make curriculum relevant to students	*Unconditional Partner* • Identify strengths, limitations, and needs • Recognize potential • Build trust through interpersonal relationships • Share your personal experience of becoming aware of different instructional strategies • Create a collaborative environment	*Director* • Encourage repeated future use of an effective instructional approach • Compliment an attempted use of an effective instructional strategy (with a specific suggestion for improvement) • Discourage future use of an ineffective instructional approach

Capacity-Building Goal: *To create awareness of the need for change and foster a desire to learn*

	Teacher's Reflective Tendencies	Related Classroom Characteristics	The Coach's Role	The Administrator's Role
Conscious Stage	• Demonstrates a consistent "knowing–doing" gap • Can ambiguously cite research to support current teaching methods • Makes excuses for problems • Demonstrates limited ability to evaluate problems • Becomes easily distracted from goals • Collaborates inconsistently with colleagues • Disregards others' ideas • Focuses first on *self*	• Instruction designed for teacher convenience • Short-term planning evident, yet inconsistent • Occasional links between instruction and assessment • Little student engagement in active, meaningful learning • Little problem solving from students • Occasional differentiation of instruction • Noticeable swings in instructional approaches	*Motivator and Strategist* • Praise generously • Reach out to include teacher in collaborative work • Communicate and maintain a clear vision • Build confidence through short-term goal setting • Focus on small changes • Make daily contact, checking in often to talk about goals and progress toward them	*Navigator* • Establish a focus for goal setting • Encourage consistency in application of effective instructional practices • Redirect teaching behaviors toward the proper heading • Extend self-reflective efforts

Capacity-Building Goal: *To motivate and show how to apply pedagogical knowledge consistently*

Teacher's Reflective Tendencies	Related Classroom Characteristics	The Coach's Role	The Administrator's Role
Action Stage			
• Accepts responsibility for the success of all students and for own personal growth • Evaluates issues and situations objectively • Seeks to incorporate research-based concepts and strategies • Reflects upon teaching only after the action • Believes in only one "right" way of doing things • Struggles to identify solutions to long-term problems • Receives feedback well, then enters a critical loop • Collaborates on a limited basis with colleagues • Focuses on the *science* of teaching	• Regular use of assessment to monitor student progress • Consistent application of best-practice instructional strategies • Lessons linked to standards • Limiting long-term planning evident • Functional at a glance, but gaps lurk	*Mentor* • Validate ideas, actions, and instructional decisions • Release responsibility and encourage independence • Provide research from which to construct meaning • Model open-mindedness toward multiple approaches and perspectives • Collaboratively engage in diagnosis and action planning	*Prompter* • Encourage reflection to support effective instructional choices • Question the impact of certain instructional strategies • Consider alternative approaches or points of view • Propose continued professional learning

Capacity-Building Goal: *To build on experience and help strengthen expertise*

Refinement Stage			
• Reflects before, during, and after taking action • Recognizes that there are multiple "right" courses of action • Maintains a vast repertoire of instructional strategies • Engages in action research as common practice • Modifies lessons and plans to meet students' needs • Pursues opportunities to work and learn with colleagues • Thinks globally, beyond the classroom • Focuses on the *art* of teaching	• Assessment drives daily instruction • Students largely responsible for their own learning • Multiple instructional strategies in use	*Collaborator* • Compliment creativity and originality • Bring attention to hard work • Stimulate discussions of personal vision and educational philosophy • Practice "mirror-listening" • Ask questions to drive personal reflection and growth	*Challenger* • Drive personal reflection • Introduce new ideas • Serve as devil's advocate • Encourage involvement in leadership

Capacity-Building Goal: *To encourage long-term growth and continued reflection*

A Teacher in the Unaware Stage: Sally

Sally was a veteran preparing to retire, but she still worked long hours in her classroom to ensure that she was ready for her students. Unfortunately, her colleagues referred to her as "stuck in her ways," and her students made few gains over the course of the first semester.

To approach her work with Sally, Alisa, in her role as instructional coach, slyly wriggled her way into Sally's classroom. She spent considerable time just building rapport and strengthening her professional relationship with Sally before requesting permission to work with some of Sally's students. Soon, she encouraged Sally to start a reflective journal and observe colleagues around the building. Using these coaching strategies suggested by Sally's stage on the Continuum of Self-Reflection, Alisa made significant headway in short order.

The part of this story we have not yet shared is the work that Pete, in his role as administrator, undertook with Sally. Taking a more directive route, he provided Sally with specific feedback during walk-throughs. At first, this feedback was generally positive—to help Sally see that the walk-through process was not a scary, "gotcha" endeavor. Then, as Alisa built upon her relationship with Sally and got her to try new teaching methods, Pete geared his feedback to encourage and compliment Sally's attempts at branching out: "It's great to see you choosing leveled texts with your students. You'll find their motivation and skills soar as you match their skills with their books!" Around this time, Pete met with Sally to set midyear goals, and he directed the conversation toward establishing a goal of investigating new methods to bolster the achievement of the students in her reading class.

Over the course of the year, Pete and Alisa shared a couple of conversations about Sally and her position on the Continuum of Self-Reflection. Because both agreed she was in the Unaware stage, Pete knew Alisa would approach Sally to attempt to break the ice. Because Pete engaged in frequent walk-throughs, Alisa knew that he would notice when she and Sally began to collaborate and share instructional strategies with her reading groups and that his feedback would encourage this to continue. The goal-setting process further strengthened the likelihood that Alisa's coaching would have a positive impact on Sally's teaching, as Pete's input helped provide the necessary focus. Together, they honed in on Sally's needs and ushered her along a pathway of professional growth.

A Teacher in the Conscious Stage: Oliver

Let's now consider Oliver, the Conscious-stage teacher who arrived at the school with a strong pedigree but without an extensive repertoire of skills. Half of his reading block consisted of spelling activities and outdated worksheets, and he failed to differentiate instruction, despite his verbalized plans to do so.

Alisa began by asking if she could try out a new teaching strategy in Oliver's classroom. She modeled a significant amount of instruction through reciprocal teaching, but Oliver had difficulty maintaining the work she had started, and he eventually began to resist making the changes. When Alisa realized his resistance came from a lack of confidence, not a lack of skill, she took a different tack. She began to make daily contact, modeled the teaching strategy, and supported him by offering short-term plans with generous praise.

Meanwhile, Pete approached his work with Oliver from a slightly different angle. Establishing a goal to increase student motivation, Pete encouraged Oliver to demonstrate consistency in his work toward increased student achievement in reading. Observing that Alisa was generating reciprocal teaching in class, Pete designed his feedback to encourage Oliver to apply his newfound knowledge: "How are you implementing reciprocal teaching on your own? When can I come in to observe students in action in your classroom?"

Early on, both of us sat down to discuss the prospect of supporting Oliver in his classroom. We recognized that there was a gap between what Oliver knew he should be doing and what he was actually practicing in his class and that this gap placed him squarely in the Conscious stage of the Continuum of Self-Reflection. As such, we agreed that Oliver needed daily contact and regular feedback to keep him on track. Alisa provided a consistent coaching plan by following the coaching strategies suggested by the Continuum, and Pete supported that work by providing specific feedback aligned with their common goal. Later on, as his proficiency grew, Oliver actually led an article study on the use of reciprocal teaching with the other teachers in his grade level.

A Teacher in the Action Stage: Meloney

Meloney was an Action-stage teacher who was a little frustrated with herself. She was committed to becoming a truly effective teacher, but she was having trouble identifying a focus. What she was looking for, in a sense, was a deficit analysis. She wanted to know what she was doing wrong so that she could fix it.

As Alisa realized that Meloney mostly needed to build confidence in the work she was doing correctly, she engaged Meloney in a reflective conversation to help her discover her strengths. At the same time, Alisa was fishing for an area in which Meloney could use some additional support. With lesson planning identified as an area of need, Alisa had her hook.

With any teacher in the Action stage, the administrator assumes the role of prompter, questioning the teacher relentlessly to encourage reflection, and that's what Pete did with Meloney. His feedback threw into sharp relief the issues she was having with lesson planning: "When and how did you plan to group students for this activity? This activity appears to have some similarities to a lesson you taught yesterday in a different subject area; how could you more closely link them together?"

In this case, both of us recognized Meloney as a teacher who was ready to take the next step to move toward the Refinement stage. To help her do that, we acknowledged that we would have to foster her curiosity and willingness to learn and act. Alisa's coaching, which included a dialogue journal, helped Meloney diagnose her work to reveal her frustrations, and Pete strategically provided her with reflective questions to help her hone her focus. With such a concentrated approach, Meloney had no choice but to grow and develop professionally.

A Teacher in the Refinement Stage: Herman

Herman was a very accommodating experienced teacher who didn't make his needs very obvious. Ultimately, he was just looking for someone to talk to. And as our conversations unfolded, it became more and more evident that Herman had a lot more to share with his colleagues than he had led us to believe.

Alisa, befuddled at first about how to support Herman, accurately assessed that he was in the Refinement stage and just needed a sounding board. After listening to him and complimenting his knowledge, Alisa proceeded to encourage him to spread his influence. Through hosting a student teacher, facilitating a book club, and opening his classroom to his peers, Herman grew professionally in a way that never would have happened without Alisa's prodding.

At the same time, it took Pete a while to identify Herman's location on the Continuum of Self-Reflection. When he did, he followed protocol by assuming the role of challenger, encouraging Herman to solidify his thinking and build his leadership capacity. When Herman ran the book club, Pete was there to provide feedback in support of the venture. In the classroom, Pete's walk-through feedback was geared to inspire deep reflection and introduce new ideas: "When you plan and debrief with your student teacher, how do you determine what was the most important thing for her to take and learn from? Are you a member of ASCD yet? There's a great article about formative assessments in the latest issue of *Educational Leadership* that I would like to discuss with you. Let's set up a time to get together."

The first thought that crossed our minds as we contemplated "the Herman enigma" was, "Really? Refinement stage? That's outstanding!" Then we got to work determining our respective plans of attack. While Alisa collaborated with Herman and established opportunities for him to share his knowledge around the building, Pete was busy bombarding him with questions to drive his reflection. As a deeply reflective person, Herman passed the challenges with flying colors.

Note the success we enjoyed with each teacher representing the four stages of the Continuum of Self-Reflection when we approached our work in tandem—not together, necessarily, but definitely as a coordinated team.

A Final Summation

We would like to end by sharing a poem that sums up our approach succinctly. It speaks to the value of self-reflection, the ability of the human brain to adapt and grow, and, well, reeks of humorous irony. Can you find the four stages of the Continuum of Self-Reflection contained therein? Give it a shot, and don't worry, there's no quiz, just a performance assessment: the successful application of your learning and reflection to your career. Good luck.

AUTOBIOGRAPHY IN FIVE SHORT CHAPTERS*
by Portia Nelson

I
I walk down the street.
There is a deep hole in the sidewalk.
I fall in.
I am lost . . . I am helpless.
It isn't my fault.
It takes forever to find a way out.

II
I walk down the same street.
There is a deep hole in the sidewalk.
I pretend I don't see it.
I fall in again.
I can't believe I am in the same place.
But, it isn't my fault.
It still takes a long time to get out.

III
I walk down the same street.
There is a deep hole in the sidewalk.
I see it there.
I still fall in . . . it's a habit.
My eyes are open.
I know where I am.
It is my fault.
I get out immediately.

IV
I walk down the same street
There is a deep hole in the sidewalk.
I walk around it.

V
I walk down another street.

References and Resources

Allington, R., & Cunningham, P. (2007). *Schools that work: Where all children read and write* (3rd ed.). Boston: Allyn & Bacon.

Allington, R., & Walmsley, S. (1995). *No quick fix: Rethinking literacy programs in America's elementary schools.* New York: Teachers College Press.

American Association for the Advancement of Science. (1909, December). The duty of the agricultural college. *Science, 30*(779), 777–789. Available: www.sciencemag.org/cgi/reprint/30/770/439 (registration required).

Angelo, T. A., & Cross, K. P. (1993). *Classroom assessment techniques: A handbook for college teachers* (2nd ed.). San Francisco: Jossey-Bass.

Archambault, R. D. (Ed.). (1974). *John Dewey on education: Selected writings.* Chicago: Chicago University Press.

Aseltine, J., Faryniarz, J., & Rigazio-DiGilio, A. (2006). *Supervision for learning: A performance-based approach to teacher development and school improvement.* Alexandria, VA: Association for Supervision and Curriculum Development.

Atherton, J. S. (2005). The experiential learning cycle. [Online article]. Available: www.learningandteaching.info/learning/experience.htm

Bailey, K., Curtis, A., & Nunan, D. (1998). Undeniable insights: Collaborative use of three professional development models. *TESOL Quarterly, 32*(3), 546–556.

Bandura, A. (1977). *Social learning theory.* Englewood Cliffs, NJ: Prentice-Hall.

Barber, M., & Mourshed, M. (2007). *How the world's best-performing school systems come out on top.* Available: www.mckinsey.com/clientservice/socialsector/resources/pdf/Worlds_School_Systems_Final.pdf

Barnes, D. (1992). The significance of teachers' frames for teaching. In T. Russell & H. Munby (Eds.), *Teachers and teaching: From classroom to reflection* (pp. 9–32). New York: Falmer Press.

Barr, A. S. (1958). Characteristics of successful teachers. *Phi Delta Kappan, 39,* 282–284.

Bartell, C. A. (2005). *Cultivating high-quality teaching through induction and mentoring.* Thousand Oaks, CA: Corwin Press.

Bellinger, G. (2004). Systems. [Online article]. Available: www.systems-thinking.org/systems/systems.htm

Bender, W., & Shores, C. (2007). *Response to intervention: A practical guide for every teacher.* Thousand Oaks, CA: Corwin Press.

Blaydes, J. (2003). *The educator's book of quotes.* Thousand Oaks, CA: Corwin Press.

Blanchard, K., Oncken, W., & Burrows, H. (1989). *The one minute manager meets the monkey.* New York: Quill William Morrow.

Boud, D., Keogh, R., & Walker, D. (1985). *Reflection: Turning experience into learning.* London: Kogan Page.

Brookfield, S. D. (1995). *Becoming a critically reflective teacher.* San Francisco: Jossey-Bass.

Brooks, H., & Russell, K. (2005). Interview. *Miracles* [Motion picture DVD]. Buena Vista Home Entertainment.

Buckingham, M. (2005). *The one thing you need to know . . . About great managing, great leading, and sustained individual success.* New York: Free Press.

Buckingham, M., & Clifton, D. O. (2001). *Now, discover your strengths.* New York: Simon & Schuster.

Buckingham, M., & Coffman, C. (1999). *First, break all the rules.* New York: Simon & Schuster.

Coleman, J. S. (1966). Equality of educational opportunity study (EEOS). ICPSR06389-v3. [Computer file.] Washington, DC: U. S. Department of Health, Education, and Welfare, Office of Education/National Center for Education Statistics [producer], 1999. Ann Arbor, MI: Inter-university Consortium for Political and Social Research [distributor], April 27, 2007.

Collins, J. (2001). *Good to great: Why some companies make the leap . . . and others don't.* New York: HarperCollins.

Comer, J. (1995). Lecture given at Education Service Center, Region IV. Houston, TX.

Coons, D. (2005). *Psychology: A modular approach to mind and behavior.* Independence, KY: Thomson Wadsworth.

Costa, A. L., & Garmston, R. J. (1994). *Cognitive coaching: A foundation for Renaissance schools.* Norwood, MA: Christopher-Gordon Publishers.

Covey, S. (1989). *The 7 habits of highly effective people.* New York: Simon & Schuster.

Covey, S. (1992). *Principle-centered leadership.* New York: Simon & Schuster.

Cross, K. P. (2001). Leading-edge efforts to improve teaching and learning: The Hesburgh Awards. *Change, 33*(4), 30–37.

Danielson, C. (2007). *Enhancing professional practice: A framework for teaching* (2nd ed.). Alexandria, VA: Association for Supervision and Curriculum Development.

Danielson, C., & McGreal, T. (2000). *Teacher evaluation to enhance professional practice.* Alexandria, VA: Association for Supervision and Curriculum Development.

Darling-Hammond, L., & McLaughlin, M. (1995). Policies that support professional development in an era of reform. *Phi Delta Kappan, 76*(8), 597–604.

Daudelin, M. W. (1996). Learning from experience through reflection. *Organizational Dynamics, 24*(3), 36–48.

Daudelin, M. W., & Hall, D. T. (1997, December). Using reflection to leverage learning. *Training and Development, 51*(12), 13–14.

Dewey, J. (1910). *How we think.* New York: Heath and Company.

Dewey, J. (1933). *How we think: A restatement of the relation of reflective thinking to the education process.* Lexington, MA: Heath and Company.

Dossey, J., McCrone, S., O'Sullivan, C., & Gonzales, P. (2006). *Problem-solving in the PISA and TIMSS 2003 assessment.* (Report No. NCES2007-049). Available: http://nces.ed.gov

Downey, C., Steffy, B., English, F., Frase, L., & Poston, W. (2004). *The three-minute classroom walk-through: Changing school supervisory practice one teacher at a time.* Thousand Oaks, CA: Corwin Press.

Drucker, P. (1999). *Management challenges of the 21st century.* New York: HarperBusiness.

DuFour, R., & Eaker, R. (1998). *Professional learning communities at work: Best practices for enhancing student achievement.* Bloomington, IN: National Educational Service.

Ershler, J. (2007). The fictive characteristics of effective educational leaders. *Academic Leadership: The Online Journal, 2*(2). Available: www.academicleadership.org/leader_action_tips/The_Fictive_Characteristics_of.shtml

Evans, R. (2001). *The human side of school change: Reform, resistance and the real-life problems of innovation.* San Francisco: Jossey-Bass.

Eyler, J., Giles, D. E., & Schmeide, A. (1996). *A practitioner's guide to reflection in service-learning: Student voices and reflections.* Nashville, TN: Vanderbilt University.

Feiman-Nemser, S., & Buchmann, M. (1987). When is student teaching teacher education? *Teaching and Teacher Education, 3*(4), 255–273.

Fiore, D., & Whitaker, T. (2005). *Six types of teachers: Recruiting, retaining and mentoring the best.* Larchmont, NY: Eye on Education.

Frase, L., & Hetzel, R. (1990). *School management by wandering around.* Lanham, MD: Scarecrow Press.

Fullan, M. (2001). *Leading in a culture of change.* San Francisco: Jossey-Bass.

Fullan, M. (2003). *The moral imperative of school leadership.* Thousand Oaks, CA: Corwin Press.

Fullan, M. (2007). *The new meaning of educational change* (4th ed.). New York: Teachers College Press.

Furlong, J., & Maynard, T. (1995). *Mentoring student teachers: The growth of professional knowledge.* London: Routledge.

Gabriel, J. (2005). *How to thrive as a teacher leader.* Alexandria, VA: Association for Supervision and Curriculum Development.

Glatthorn, A. (1997). *Differentiated supervision* (2nd ed.). Alexandria, VA: Association for Supervision and Curriculum Development.

Glickman, C. (1990). *Supervision of instruction.* Boston: Allyn & Bacon.

Graf, O., & Werlinich, J. (2003). *Differentiated supervision and professional development: Using multiple vehicles to drive teaching & learning from good to great.* Paper presented at the Principal's Academy of Western Pennsylvania, Pittsburgh, PA.

Greenleaf, R. (1970). *The servant as leader.* Indianapolis: The Robert Greenleaf Center.

Greenleaf, R. (2003). *The servant leader within: A transformative path.* Mahwah, NJ: Paulist Press.

Greenleaf, R., & Spears, L. C. (2002). *Servant leadership: A journey into the nature of legitimate power and greatness.* Mahwah, NJ: Paulist Press.

Grigg, W., Donahue, P., & Dion, G. (2007). *The nation's report card: Twelfth grade reading and mathematics.* (Report No. NCES2007-468). Available: http://nces.ed.gov

Guskin, A. (1994). Reducing student costs and enhancing student learning: Restructuring the role of the faculty. *Change, 26*(5), 16–25.

Gustafson, K., & Bennett, W. (1999). *Issues and difficulties in promoting learner reflection: Results from a three-year study.* Available: http://it.coe.uga.edu/~kgustafs/document/promoting.html

Hall, G., & Hord, S. (2000). *Implementing change: Patterns, principles, and potholes.* Boston: Allyn and Bacon.

Hall, P. (2004). *The first-year principal.* Lanham, MD: Rowman & Littlefield.

Hall, P. (2005a, February). A school reclaims itself. *Educational Leadership, 62*(5), 70–73.

Hall, P. (2005b). The principal's presence and supervision to improve teaching. *SEDL Letter, 17*(2), 12–16.

Hall, P. (2006a). Get out of that chair! *Education World.* Available: www.educationworld.com/a_admin/columnists/hall/hall006.shtml

Hall, P. (2006b). Prioritize and delegate your way to effective leadership. *Education World.* Available: www.educationworld.com/a_admin/columnists/hall/hall007.shtml

Hall, P. (2006c). T2: Togetherness and teamwork. *Education World.* Available: www.education-world.com/a_admin/columnists/hall/hall011.shtml

Hall, P. (2007). Turning teacher evaluations on their ears. *Education World.* Available: www.educationworld.com/a_admin/columnists/hall/hall016.shtml

Hall, P. (2008a). Building bridges: Strengthening the principal induction process through intentional mentoring. *Phi Delta Kappan, 89*(6), 449–452.

Hall, P. (2008b). Leading off the edge of the map. *Education World.* Available: www.education-world.com/a_admin/columnists/hall/hall023.shtml

Harland, P. (1999, June). The "mirror model." [Online article]. Available: www.cleanlanguage.co.uk//articles/articles/95/1/The-Mirror-Model/Page1.html

Harris, S. (1981). *Know yourself? It's a paradox.* Associated Press.

Harris, S. (2005). *Best practices of award-winning elementary school principals.* Thousand Oaks, CA: Corwin Press.

Harvey, T. R. (1995). *Checklist for change: A pragmatic approach to creating and controlling change* (2nd ed.). Boston: Allyn & Bacon.

Harvey, T. R., & Drolet, B. (1995). *Building teams, building people: Expanding the fifth resource* (2nd ed.). Lancaster, CA: Technomic Publishing.

Hatton, N., & Smith, D. (1995). Reflection in teacher education: Towards definition and implementation. [Online article]. Available: http:/alex.edfac.usyd.edu.au/LocalResource/Study1/hattonart.html

Haycock, K. (1998). Good teaching matters . . . a lot. *Thinking K–16, 3*(2), 1–14.

Heifetz, R. (1994). *Leadership without easy answers.* Cambridge, MA: The Belknap Press of Harvard University Press.

Henderson, J. G. (1992). *Reflective teaching: Becoming an inquiring educator.* New York: Macmillan.

Henderson, J. G. (1996). *Reflective teaching: The study of your constructivist practices.* Englewood Cliffs, NJ: Merrill Prentice-Hall.

Hertling, E. (2000). Evaluating the results of whole-school reform. *ERIC Digest Number 140.* Available: http://findarticles.com/p/articles/mi_pric/is_200009/ai_2819410239

Hoare, C. H. (2006). *Handbook of adult development and learning.* New York: Oxford University Press.

Hoerr, T. (2008, December/January). What is instructional leadership? *Educational Leadership, 65*(4), 84–85.

Hoff, D. (2007). Turnarounds central issue under NCLB. *Education Week, 26*(42), 32–33.

Hoover, L. (1994). Reflective writing as a window on preservice teachers' thought processes. *Teaching and Teacher Education, 10*(1), 83–93.

Hopkins, G. (2007). Walk-throughs are on the move. *Education World.* Available: www.education-world.com/a_admin/admin/admin405.shtml

Janas, M. (1996, Fall). Mentoring the mentor: A challenge for staff development. *Journal of Staff Development, 17*(4), 2–5.

Jarvis, P. (1987). *Adult learning in the social context.* London: Croom Helm.

Johnston, H. (2001). Leadership by walking around: Walkthroughs and instructional improvement. [Online article]. Available: www.principalspartnership.com/feature203.html

Jordan, H. R., Mendro, R. L., & Weersinghe, D. (1997). *Teacher effects on longitudinal student achievement: A preliminary report on research on teacher effectiveness.* Paper presented at the National Evaluation Institute, Indianapolis, IN.

Katzenbach, J. R., & Smith, D. K. (1993). *The wisdom of teams: Creating the high-performance organization.* New York: HarperCollins.

Keller, B. (2008). Drive on to improve evaluation systems for teachers. *Education Week, 27*(19), 8.

Kerry, T., & Mayes, A. S. (1995). *Issues in mentoring*. New York: Routledge.

King, P. M., & Kitchener, K. S. (1994). *Developing reflective judgment: Understanding and promoting intellectual growth and critical thinking in adolescents and adults*. San Francisco: Jossey-Bass.

Kise, J. (2006). *Differentiated coaching: A framework for helping teachers change*. Thousand Oaks, CA: Corwin Press.

Kitchener, K. S., & Fischer, K. W. (1990). A skill approach to the development of reflective thinking. In D. Kuhn (Ed.), *Contributions to human development* (Vol. 21). *Developmental perspectives on teaching and learning* (pp. 48–62). Basel, Switzerland: Karger.

Knight, J. (2004). Instructional coaches make progress through partnership. *Journal of Staff Development, 25*(2), 32–37.

Knight, J. (2007). *Instructional coaching: A partnership approach for improving instruction*. Thousand Oaks, CA: Corwin Press.

Kolb, D. A. (1984). *Experiential learning: Experience as the source of learning and development*. Englewood Cliffs, NJ: Prentice-Hall.

Kruger, J., & Dunning, D. (1999). Unskilled and unaware of it: How difficulties in recognizing one's own incompetence lead to inflated self-assessments. *Journal of Personality and Social Psychology, 77*(6), 1121–1134.

Learning Point Associates. (2007). Using the classroom walk-through as an instructional leadership strategy. [Online article]. Available: www.centerforcsri.org/index.php?option=com_content&task=view&id=424&Itemid=5

Lee, J., Grigg, W., & Donahue, P. (2007). *The nation's report card: Reading 2007*. (Report No. NCES2007-496). Washington, DC: National Center for Education Statistics, Institute of Education Sciences, U.S. Department of Education.

Liesveld, R., Miller, J., & Robison, J. (2005). *Teach with your strengths: How great teachers inspire their students*. New York: Gallup Press.

Lipton, L., & Wellman, B. (2007, September). How to talk so teachers listen. *Educational Leadership, 65*(1), 30–34.

Liston, D., & Zeichner, K. (1996). *Reflective teaching: An introduction*. Mahwah, NJ: Lawrence Erlbaum Associates.

Loughran, J. J. (1996). *Developing reflective practice: Learning about teaching and learning through modeling*. London: Routledge.

Lynch, C. L. (1996). Facilitating and assessing unstructured problem solving. *Journal of College Reading and Learning, 27*, 16–27.

Lynch, C. L., Wolcott, S. K., & Huber, G. E. (2001). Steps for better thinking skill patterns. [Online article]. Available: www.idea.ksu.edu/papers/Idea_Paper_37.pdf

Lyons, C. A., & Pinnell, G. S. (2001). *Systems for change in literacy education: A guide to professional development*. Portsmouth, NH: Heinemann.

Marshall, K. (2005). It's time to rethink teacher supervision and evaluation. *Phi Delta Kappan, 86*(10), 727–735.

Marshall, K. (2006). What's a principal to do? *Education Week, 86*(1), 17.

Marzano, R. J. (2003). *What works in schools: Translating research into action*. Alexandria, VA: Association for Supervision and Curriculum Development.

Marzano, R. J. (2007). *The art and science of teaching*. Alexandria, VA: Association for Supervision and Curriculum Development.

Marzano, R. J., Pickering, D. J., & Pollock, J. E. (2001). *Classroom instruction that works: Research-based strategies for increasing student achievement*. Alexandria, VA: Association for Supervision and Curriculum Development.

Marzano, R., Waters, T., & McNulty, B. (2005). *School leadership that works: From research to results*. Alexandria, VA: Association for Supervision and Curriculum Development.

Maslow, A. H. (1962). *Toward a psychology of being.* Princeton, NJ: Van Nostrand

Maurer, R. (2007). Resistance to change: Why it matters and what to do about it. [Online article]. Available: www.beyondresistance.com/resistance_to_change.htm

McCarthy, M. D. (1996). One-time and short-term service learning experiences. In B. Jacoby & Associates (Eds.), *Service-learning in higher education* (pp. 113–134). San Francisco: Jossey-Bass.

McEwan, E. K. (2001). *10 traits of highly effective teachers: How to hire, coach, and mentor successful teachers.* Thousand Oaks, CA: Corwin Press.

McKeever, B. (2003). *Nine lessons of successful school leadership teams.* San Francisco: WestEd.

Miner, B. (2005/2006, Winter). Does improved teacher quality lead to improved student learning? *Rethinking Schools Online,* 20(2). Available: www.rethinkingschools.org/archive/20_02/lead202.shtml

Moran, M. C. (2007). *Differentiated literacy coaching: Scaffolding for student and teacher success.* Alexandria, VA: Association for Supervision and Curriculum Development.

Murray, J. (2005). Why faculty development? Enhancing faculty development in the community college. Available: www.texascollaborative.org/MurrayAug05/need.php

National Association of Elementary School Principals. (2008). *Leading learning communities: Standards for what principals should know and be able to do.* Alexandria, VA: Author.

National Commission on Excellence in Education. (1983). *A nation at risk: The imperative for educational reform.* Washington, DC: U.S. Government Printing Office.

Nevada Department of Education. (2005). *Innovation and the prevention of remediation.* Carson City, NV: State of Nevada.

Oates, S. B. (1994). *With malice toward none: A life of Abraham Lincoln.* New York: Harper Perennial.

Osterman, K. F., & Kottkamp, R. B. (2004). *Reflective practice for educators.* Thousand Oaks, CA: Corwin Press.

Payne, R. K. (2005). *A framework for understanding poverty.* Highlands, TX: aha! Process, Inc.

Perry, W. G. (1981). Cognitive and ethical growth: The making of meaning. In A. W. Chickering & Associates (Eds.), *The modern American college* (pp. 76–116). San Francisco: Jossey-Bass.

Perry, W. G. (1998). *Forms of intellectual and ethical development in the college years: A scheme.* New York: Holt, Rinehart, and Winston.

Pfeffer, J., & Sutton, R. I. (2000). *The knowing–doing gap: How smart companies turn knowledge into action.* Boston: President and Fellows of Harvard College.

Pianta, R., Belsky, J., Houts, R., & Morrison, F. (2007). Opportunities to learn in America's elementary classrooms. *Science,* 315(5820), 1795–1796.

Pollard, A. (2002). *Readings for reflective teaching.* New York: Continuum International Publishing Group.

Porter, J. E. (2006). *Promoting the success of individual learners.* Charlotte, NC: Information Age Publishing.

Reason, C., & Reason, L. (2007, September). Asking the right questions. *Educational Leadership,* 84(1), 36–40.

Reeves, D. B. (2006, November). Leading to change: Preventing 1,000 failures. *Educational Leadership,* 64(3), 88–89.

Rethinking Schools Online. (2005/2006, Winter). Getting to the heart of quality teaching. *Rethinking Schools Online,* 20(2). Available: www.rethinkingschools.org/archive/20_02/edit202.shtml

Richardson, J. (2001). Seeing through new eyes: Walk throughs offer new way to view schools. [Online article]. Available: www.nsdc.org/library/publications/tools/tools10-01rich.cfm

Richardson, V. (1998). How teachers change: What will lead to change that most benefits student learning? *Focus on Basics,* 2(C). Available: www.ncsall.net/?id=395

Rosenholtz, S. J. (1991). *Teachers' workplace: The social organization of schools.* New York: Teachers College Press.

Rutherford, R. B., Quinn, M. M., & Mathur, S. R. (2007). *Handbook of research in emotional and behavioral disorders.* New York: Guilford Press.

Sack, J. (2002). Experts debate effect of whole school reform. *Education Week, 21*(20), 6.

Sagor, R. (1991, March). What project LEARN reveals about collaborative action research. *Educational Leadership, 49*(6), 6–10.

Scheeler, M., Ruhl, K., & McAfee, J. (2004). Providing performance feedback to teachers: A review. *Teacher Education and Special Education, 27*(3), 311–323.

Schmoker, M. (1999). *Results: The key to continuous school improvement* (2nd ed.). Alexandria, VA: Association for Supervision and Curriculum Development.

Schmoker, M. (2004). Tipping point: From feckless reform to substantive instructional improvement. *Phi Delta Kappan, 85*(6), 424–432.

Schmoker, M. (2006). *Results now: How we can achieve unprecedented improvements in teaching and learning.* Alexandria, VA: Association for Supervision and Curriculum Development.

Schön, D. A. (1983). *The reflective practitioner: How professionals think in action.* New York: Basic Books.

Schön, D. A. (1987). *Educating the reflective practitioner.* San Francisco: Jossey-Bass.

Schuler, A. J. (2003). Overcoming resistance to change: Top ten reasons for change resistance. *What's Up, Doc?; Schuler Solutions Newsletter, 3*(9). Available: www.schulersolutions.com/resistance_to_change.html

Secretan, L. (2004). *Inspire! What great leaders do.* Hoboken, NJ: John Wiley & Sons.

Seifert, K. L. (1999). *Reflective thinking and professional development.* Boston: Houghton Mifflin.

Showers, B., Murphy, C., & Joyce, B. (1996). The River City program: Staff development becomes school improvement. In B. Joyce and E. Calhoun (Eds.), *Learning experiences in school renewal: An exploration of five successful programs* (pp. 13–51). Eugene, OR: ERIC Clearinghouse on Educational Management. (ERIC Document Reproduction Service No. ED 401 600)

Stiggins, R. (2004a, May). All about accountability: Those {fill-in-the-blank} tests! *Educational Leadership, 63*(8), 85–86.

Stiggins, R. (2004b). New assessment beliefs for a new school mission. *Phi Delta Kappan, 86*(1), 22–27.

Stoll, L., Fink, D., & Earl, L. M. (2003). *It's about learning (and it's about time).* New York: Routledge.

Storms, B. A., Riazantseva, A., & Gentile, C. (2000). Focusing in on content and communication. *California English, 5*(4), 26–27.

Sturtevant, E. G. (2003). *The literacy coach: A key to improving teaching and learning in secondary schools.* Washington, DC: The Alliance for Excellent Education.

Toll, C. (2005). *The literacy coach's survival guide: Essential questions and practical answers.* Washington, DC: International Reading Association.

United States Department of Education. (2006). *The Reading First program's grant application process: Final inspection report.* Washington, DC: Office of the Inspector General.

Valli, L. (1992). *Reflective teacher education: Cases and critiques.* Albany: State University of New York Press.

Van Manen, J. (1977). Linking ways of knowing with ways of being practical. *Curriculum Inquiry, 6,* 205–208.

Viadro, D. (2007). No easy answers about NCLB's effect on "poverty gap." *Education Week, 27*(12), 12.

Wallis, C., & Steptoe, S. (2006, December 10). How to bring our schools out of the 20th century. *Time,* 50–56.

Wasley, P. A. (1992). Working together: Teacher leadership and collaboration. In Carol Livingston (Ed.), *Teachers as leaders: Evolving roles.* Washington, DC: National Education Association.

Werlinich, J. (2003, August). Walk-throughs as professional practice: A workshop for administrators and school leaders in the Washoe County School District, Reno, Nevada.

Whitaker, T. (2003). *What great principals do differently: Fifteen things that matter most.* Larchmont, NY: Eye on Education.

Wilhelm, J. D. (2001). *Improving instruction with think-aloud strategies.* New York: Scholastic, Inc.

Wolcott, S. K., & Lynch, C. L. (1997). Critical thinking in the accounting classroom: A reflective judgment development process perspective. *Accounting Education, 2*(1), 59–78.

Wong, H. K., & Wong, R. T. (1998). *The first days of school: How to be an effective teacher.* Mountain View, CA: Harry K. Wong Publications.

Wood, F. H. (2007). *Handbook of research in emotional and behavioral disorders.* New York: Guilford Press.

Wood, J. T. (2005). *Communication in our lives.* Independence, KY: Thomson Wadsworth.

Yinger, R., & Clark, M. (1981). *Reflective journal writing: Theory and practice.* East Lansing: Michigan State University, Institute for Research on Teaching.

Zeichner, K. M., & Liston, D. P. (1996). *Reflective teaching: An introduction.* Philadelphia: Lawrence Erlbaum Associates.

Zmuda, A., Kuklis, R., & Kline, E. (2004). *Transforming schools: Creating a culture of continuous improvement.* Alexandria, VA: Association for Supervision and Curriculum Development.

Zmuda, A., Kuklis, R., & Kline, E. (2005). *Qualified teachers for at-risk schools: A national imperative.* Washington, DC: National Partnership for Teaching in At-Risk Schools.

Index

Note: The letter *f* following a page number denotes a figure.

About the Authors

Pete Hall is the principal of Sheridan Elementary School in Spokane, Washington, a Title I school whose recent academic successes have been recognized by the Office of the Superintendent of Public Instruction in Washington. ASCD's Outstanding Young Educator Award honoree for 2004, Mr. Hall gained international recognition for his work as the principal of Anderson Elementary School in Reno, Nevada, a high-poverty Title I school that went from failing to make adequate yearly progress under the No Child Left Behind Act for four consecutive years to earning a "High Achieving" designation.

Mr. Hall has worked in the U.S. public school system for 13 years, 9 of them as a school administrator. He is the author of a dozen articles and books on educational leadership, as well as a presenter and consultant. His teaching experience includes primary elementary, intermediate elementary, and middle school. He and his wife live with their three beautiful children in Coeur d'Alene, Idaho. He can be reached at (208) 755-3139 or via e-mail at petehall@educationhall.com.

Alisa Simeral is the literacy coach at Anderson Elementary School in Reno, Nevada. She was awarded the International Reading Association's Celebrate Literacy Award in 2006 and the Washoe Education Association Distinguished Performance Award in 2008. Mrs. Simeral's work has been instrumental in transforming several low-performing schools into hubs of literate, thoughtful students.

Mrs. Simeral's varied experiences in education have led her through California, Alaska, Arizona, and Nevada, and she has served as a primary elementary teacher, intermediate elementary teacher, and literacy coach. A seasoned consultant and presenter at conferences and workshops for educators, she has spoken at national conferences for ASCD and the National Staff Development Council, as well as at numerous statewide, local, and district events. She and her husband live with their two wonderful children in old southwest Reno. She can be reached at (775) 772-7683 or via e-mail at asimeral@washoe.k12.nv.us.